CREATIVE**INTERVALLIC** **GUITAR**SOLOING

Master the Art of Using Interval Skips To Play More Creative Rock Guitar Solos

SHAUN**BAXTER**

FUNDAMENTAL**CHANGES**

Creative Intervallic Guitar Soloing

Master the Art of Using Interval Skips To Play More Creative Rock Guitar Solos

ISBN: 978-1-78933-446-3

Published by **www.fundamental-changes.com**

Copyright © 2024 Shaun Baxter

Edited by Joseph Alexander & Tim Pettingale

www.fundamental-changes.com

For over 350 free guitar lessons with videos check out:

www.fundamental-changes.com

Join our free Facebook Community of Cool Musicians

www.facebook.com/groups/fundamentalguitar

All audio recorded and mixed at Brakenhurst Studios by Shaun Baxter

All transcriptions by Shaun Baxter

Cover Image Copyright: Shaun Baxter

Contents

About the Author

Shaun Baxter is a world-renowned guitar player and the UK's most experienced and respected rock guitar teacher.

He was a founder member of The Guitar Institute in London in 1986 (which was partnered with the London College of Music and became the biggest trade-school for guitar in Europe) where he taught every week for over 20 years. He went on to be Head of Guitar at Guitar-X in London before, in 2003, becoming an owner and the Academic Director of The Academy of Music and Sound (AMS), a national network of musical schools, opening centres all over the UK. At one point, via their various apprenticeship schemes, AMS were the biggest employer in the Scottish music industry and their alumni includes Lewis Capaldi.

Shaun composed the world's first Grade 8 Guitar syllabus for Trinity College, wrote the UK's National Operational Standards (NOS) for music performance, and contributed to magazines such as *The Guitar Magazine*, *Guitar World*, *Metal Hammer* and *Guitar Techniques* (for whom he wrote a popular and influential monthly column for 27 years).

Through his teaching, Shaun helped to pioneer popular music education in the UK and taught many high profile guitarists such as Rick Graham, Andy James, Jon Gomm and Justin Sandercoe, as well as many others who have found fame with artists such as Public Image Ltd, Asia, Craig David, Moby, Wynton Marsalis, Haken, Martin Taylor, Steve Hackett, Rick Wakeman, Mike Oldfield, The Art of Noise, Leo Sayer, Pet Shop Boys, Roger Waters and Queen.

During the '90s, he was a member of the Composition Department at the London College of Music and also lectured at Brunel University, Leeds College of Music, University of West London, Bath Spa University, Coventry University and Rostock University of Music and Drama in Germany.

In 1993, Shaun recorded his ground-breaking *Jazz Metal* solo album.

He has performed with players such as Uli Jon Roth (Scorpions), Neil Murray (Whitesnake, Black Sabbath), and Ron "Bumblefoot" Thal (Guns & Roses), and also toured the world and/or recorded with artists such as Princess, John Sloman (Gary Moore/Uriah Heep), Todd Rundgren and Carl Palmer of Emerson Lake and Palmer.

"He is one of the greatest musicians I have played with." (Carl Palmer, legendary progressive rock drummer).

As an artist, he has been an official endorsee of Marshall Amplification, Cornford Amplification, Fender Guitars, Patrick Eggle Guitars, Line 6 effects, Two-Note Audio Engineering, and Picato Strings.

Finally, Shaun was one of only eight heavy metal guitar players (along with Edward Van Halen, Joe Satriani, Steve Vai, Yngwie Malmsteen, Nuno Bettencourt, Michael Schenker and Paul Gilbert) featured in the world's biggest-selling music book, *Guitar: A Complete Guide for the Player* (2002).

Shaun appeared in a list of "the top 50 rock guitar players since the 1980s" in *Guitarist* magazine and was also included in *The Guitarist's Book of Guitarist Players* (1994) which details "the world's most influential guitarists and bass players". His album, *Jazz Metal* topped its 50 recommended fusion guitar recordings.

Shaun is the bestselling author of the guitar methods *Chromatic Lead Guitar Techniques*, and *Dominant Pentatonic Guitar Soloing* published by **www.Fundamental-Changes.com**

Introduction

An *interval* is a term that describes the distance between two different notes. As soon as you play two different pitches, you've created an interval.

Intervals are named after the musical distance they create and these names and distances are shown in the table below. Don't feel the need to memorise this now, but you can refer back to this table at any time.

INTERVAL DISTANCES	
SIMPLE INTERVALS (Interval name in first octave)	Distance in tones (T) and semitones (½)
b2	½
2	T
#2 or b3	T + ½
3	T + T
4	T + T + ½
#4 or b5	T + T + T
5	T + T + T + ½
#5 or b6	T + T + T + T
6	T + T + T + T + ½
b7	T + T + T + T + T
7	T + T + T + T + T + ½
Octave	T + T + T + T + T + T
COMPOUND INTERVALS (Equivalent notes an octave higher)	
b9	Octave + ½
9	Octave + T
#9 or b10	Octave + T + ½
10	Octave + T + T
11	Octave + T + T + ½
#11 or b12	Octave + T + T + T
12	Octave + T + T + T + ½
#12 or b13	Octave + T + T + T + T
13	Octave + T + T + T + T + ½
b14	Octave + T + T + T + T + T
14	Octave + T + T + T + T + T + ½
15 (Double Octave)	Octave + T + T + T + T + T + T

Why Intervals Are Important

Using intervals in our playing is a great way of developing approaches that produce distinctive musical effects. Each interval type has its own innate flavour (fourths and fifths sound quite hard and modern, whereas thirds and sixths sound softer, poppier and often country tinged), and this is something we can use to our advantage to control the mood of what we play when improvising.

The Aim of This Book

The aim of this book is to inspire you to go beyond the basics of interval exploration, and show you how various interval types can be extracted from a scale and used when improvising to create ear-catching lines.

This book does *not* cover rudimentary exercises, well-worn guitar clichés, or intervals applied to every conceivable scale. For a more comprehensive approach to the basics of intervals and soloing with patterns, check out *Guitar Fretboard Fluency* by Joseph Alexander.

This book is written for the more advanced guitarist who already has a foundational understanding of intervals and how to use them. Here, we will study ten solos crammed with advanced applications of intervallic material, and you will learn concepts that will act as inspiration for your further exploration, as you write your own licks, lines and solos.

Whenever you hear an approach you like in a solo, apply it to every shape of every other scale you know. This will cement the effect of the intervallic leap into your musical vocabulary and you will be able to draw on it on any occasion.

Diatonic Intervals

A *diatonic* interval means one that is related to, or derived from, a scale. In other words, it refers to a series of notes that exist entirely *within* the scale.

Playing a series of diatonic intervals requires us to adapt the shape of the interval on the neck when playing it from different notes to ensure that the notes remain in the scale. Thankfully, this is much easier to visualise and do in practice than it is to describe in words.

Once you've learned what a particular interval type looks like, you no longer need to use theory to play that diatonic interval in the scale – the process is purely visual. Let's take a random interval – a sixth, for example. The diagram below shows sixth intervals in the A Mixolydian scale. Play through them enough times and you'll quickly learn to visualise them on the fretboard. Once you've learned the shapes, it's simply a matter of joining the dots as shown.

Like any mode of the major scale, Mixolydian has only two types of diatonic sixth: major and minor. In the diagram below, the major sixths are grey and the minor sixths are black.

Diatonic Sixths in A Mixolydian

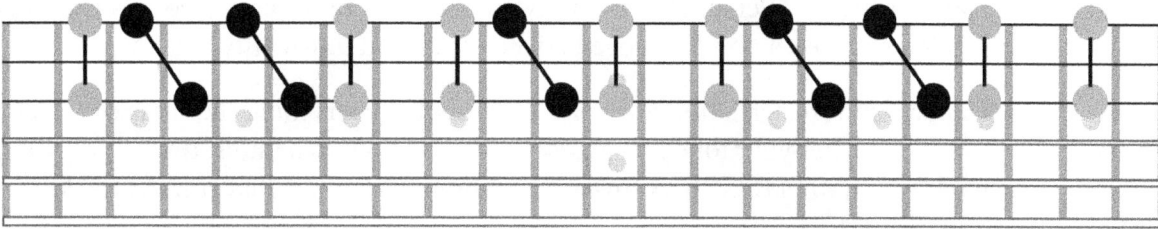

Side Note: Sometimes confusion arises when chord types have the same names as intervals, e.g., "seventh chords". In this book, whenever you see words like sixth, seventh etc., they *always* refer to the interval distance.

As you begin to visualise each interval type along the neck, work at learning to "zoom out" to see as much of the scale as possible. In other words, develop the skill of being able to see as much of the scale as possible *beforehand*, so you know exactly where you're heading, rather than unveiling each new area at the last moment before you play it.

My Approach to the Solo Studies

This book uses a series of solo studies played over the same backing track. Each study is a cornucopia of useful sequences and lines that will expand your intervallic soloing options. By learning these ideas in the context of a solo (as opposed to isolated exercises or lines), you will get a chance to hear each intervallic idea in action and better understand the feel each one creates.

Many of the ideas here originated on paper first, often derived via a systematic approach based on note order and fingering (an overview of my approach is included in the Appendix of this book). I began by auditioning each idea (and there were hundreds), programming them into a sequencer, and selecting my favourites. This process allowed me to assess each idea objectively, as if someone else was playing it, without me having to learn it first! The resulting ideas formed the musical palette for composing each solo and often involved a compromise between tonal quality and playing ease.

Once I could play the ideas, I used them to improvise over the backing track. In other words, I responded to the backing music, playing specific ideas using a particular guitar sound in the moment, as part of a natural process, rather than playing them as pre-written ideas. The results were inevitably more human, balanced and personal. Improvised passages always have a better use of space and a more natural way of entering and exiting each idea. Forcing ourselves to play pre-written ideas feels like hammering a square peg into a round hole and the results are never as good.

To choose the solos that would make it into this book, I listened to multiple recordings of my improvisations, and selected the ones I liked best. If you copy this process you will end up with passages that already sound good in their musical context. Exploring each idea through improvisation will also improve your ability to get into the musical "zone" – that magical, creative, spontaneous mindset where the ideas just flow.

When you study something new, the concept flows from the page to your head. This is the process of *understanding*. However, through practice, you can internalise the concept so that it flows musically from your brain to your audience via your fingers. Personally, I simply focus on trying to create some beauty and expression, and that definitely helps me keep a good balance between craft and musicality.

Although I show my technical approach for each solo, you don't have to play everything the same way as me. Lean into your strengths but always consider your tone and phrasing. Think about dynamics, timing and tuning accuracy. Does your approach allow you to play with expression and produce sounds that suit the track?

Every intervallic soloing approach in this book can (and should, if you like it!) be applied to every scale, so we are going to learn these ideas on a single scale type to start. Every solo study is played over a backing track that involves playing only the Mixolydian scale from just two different root notes (A and C). When you hear an idea you like in any of the solos, you should learn it in other scales too.

The chart below shows the chord changes to the backing track we'll be playing over and indicates where each Mixolydian scale is used.

A Mixolydian (A, B, C#, D, E, F#, G) --			
A	A	G/A	G/A
			(x2)
C Mixolydian (C, D, E, F, G, A, Bb)---			
Bbadd9	F	C	C
			(x4)

It's vital that you download and listen to the audio examples to get a full sense of what the concepts have to offer. Don't just learn the ideas from the page. The pages are just a way of demystifying the music but the audio is where it all starts.

Download the audio now at **www.fundamental-changes.com**

Get the Audio

The audio files for this book are available to download for free from **www.fundamental-changes.com.** The link is in the top right-hand corner. Click on the "Guitar" link then simply select this book title from the drop-down menu and follow the instructions to get the audio.

We recommend that you download the files directly to your computer, not to your tablet, and extract them there before adding them to your media library.

For over 350 free guitar lessons with videos check out:

www.fundamental-changes.com

Join our free Facebook Community of Cool Musicians

www.facebook.com/groups/fundamentalguitar

Tag us for a share on Instagram: **FundamentalChanges**

Chapter One: Second Intervals Solo Study

Musical Effect

Second intervals are simply consecutive scale steps, so there's nothing particularly striking about their sound. However, when played as double-stops, the close proximity of pitches creates a dissonant effect, particularly when played with distortion, and even more so when the interval is a minor second (two notes a semitone apart).

Musical Considerations

Although they are good for musical balance, it is vital to combine second intervals with wider ones to create interesting melodies. It's natural for most guitar players to play scales by moving up or down to the next note in a scale, but that condemns us to always playing *steps* rather than *leaps*. The latter always sounds more interesting and the fusion guitarist and educator Scott Henderson has often admonished students by saying, "Do you *just* play semitones and tones?!"

However, we won't overlook second intervals because they often constitute an important part of the overall mix of elements in any solo, and there are ways of using extended technique to expand their use.

Solo Performance Notes

If there are any second-based sequences in the following solo study that capture your imagination, extract them and apply them to every shape of any other scale that you know.

For ease of reading on guitar, the transcription for this and every other solo study in this book is written in 4/4, rather than 6/8. If your rhythm reading isn't great don't worry, just use the tablature and your ears to match the notation to the rhythms on the audio track.

In the transcription you'll notice that some notes have rectangular boxes around them.

- Rectangle around two notes = a single diatonic second interval

- Rectangle around three or more notes = multiple consecutive diatonic second intervals

Bars 1-6

Bar 3 features second intervals (three-note cells) shifted laterally along the length of the high E string in A Mixolydian. Rhythmically, these are "nested" tuplets that require you to focus on tracing out a 1/4 note triplet rhythm with the first note of each 1/8th note triplet.

This is followed by a descending A Minor Blues scale line in bars 4-5 before an ascending A Major Pentatonic scale line in bar 6 created from the following three-octave symmetrical fingering.

A Major Pentatonic Scale (3-Octave Symmetrical Shape)

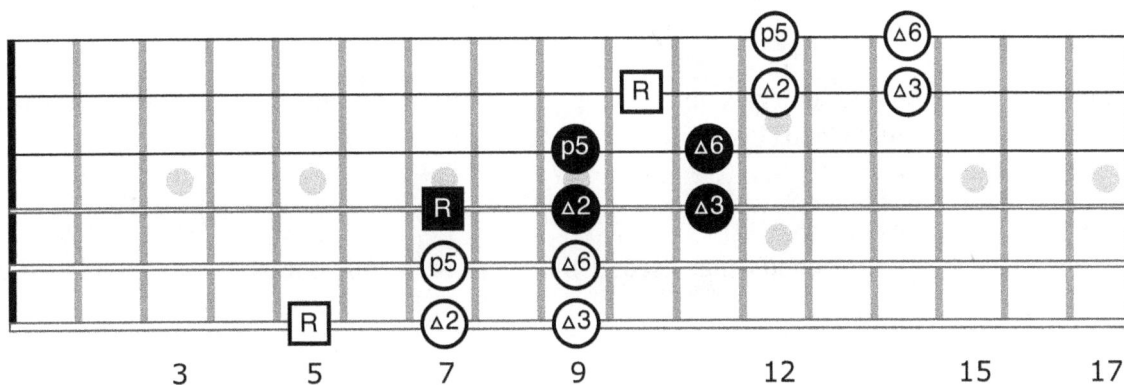

Bars 7-10

In bar 7, we explore of the characteristic grinding dissonance created when groups of seconds are played simultaneously on adjacent strings. You don't have to use the hybrid picking pattern written in the transcription, but it may help to give more snap to certain notes.

Bar 8 features a series of ascending seconds played to a triplet count that produces a "2 against 3" rhythmic feel. This approach can also be seen in bars 12, 27 and 33. Consecutive seconds are continued throughout the bulk of bars 9 & 10 and are also used in bars 13-16, 17-20, 35-36, 43, and 45.

Bars 11-12

This passage picks out various second intervals from a hexatonic (six-note) scale that exists in Mixolydian. Omit the b7 of C Mixolydian to create the C Major Hexatonic scale with the spelling 1, 2, 3, 4, 5, 6.

C Major Hexatonic Scale

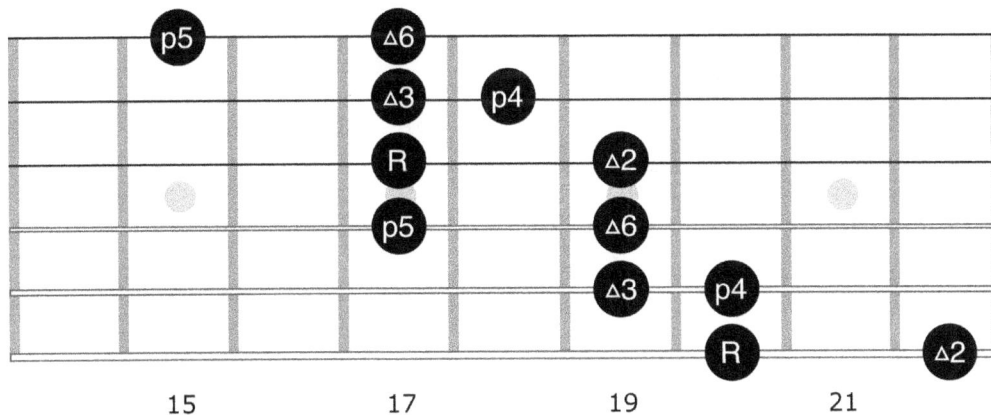

Bar 11 contains a series of three-note cells, and more interest is created by using string skips in bar 12, an approach also used in bars 23-24 and 39.

Bars 21-24

This section doesn't really feature second intervals and is simply a link between those passages that do. Apart from the D note, bars 22-24 consist of a Cadd11 arpeggio (1, 3, 4, 5).

Bars 25-28

Bar 27 features a series of descending seconds that ascend the scale in 1/16th notes. These are played in CAGED Shape 4 of A Mixolydian.

Bars 29-32

Bar 30 contains a series of ascending four-note cells of consecutive seconds that move up through the scale. Bar 31 contains the opposite (descending cells moving down through the scale). When played in triplets these four-note cells become rhythmically displaced, similar to any two-note motif, in this case producing a "four against three" effect that helps the passage to sound less repetitive.

Bar 32 contains a descending A major triad that finishes on a b7th (G).

Bars 33-40

Bar 33 features a series of ascending second intervals that descend the scale – the opposite of bar 27.

Apart from the D note in bar 39, bars 39-40 use the notes of F Ionian Pentatonic, 1, 3, 4, 5, 7 (F, A, Bb, C, E), which exists within C Mixolydian.

F Ionian Pentatonic

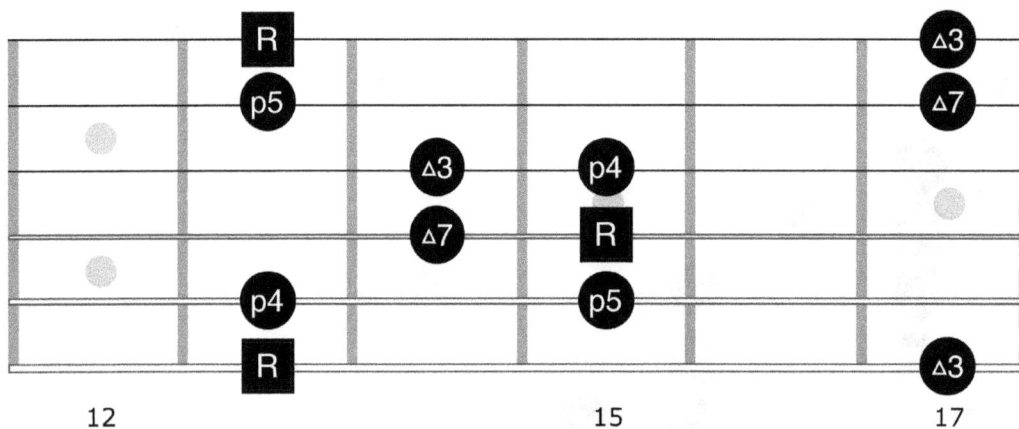

Bars 41-42

Here, various second units and cells shift down the string against a tapped pedal/pivot note. The numbers in brackets indicate rhythmic groupings.

Bars 46-48

Bar 46 starts with a typical example of the dissonance of a semitone double-stop (a second interval where both notes are held down simultaneously).

In bar 47 we use ascending four-note cells that descend the scale as a variation on the approach used in bars 30 and 31.

TWICE AS NICE
(Solo Study Featuring Second Intervals)

Bbadd9
F
Consecutive seconds
C
Bbadd9
F
C
Consecutive seconds
BU
Bbadd9
Consecutive seconds

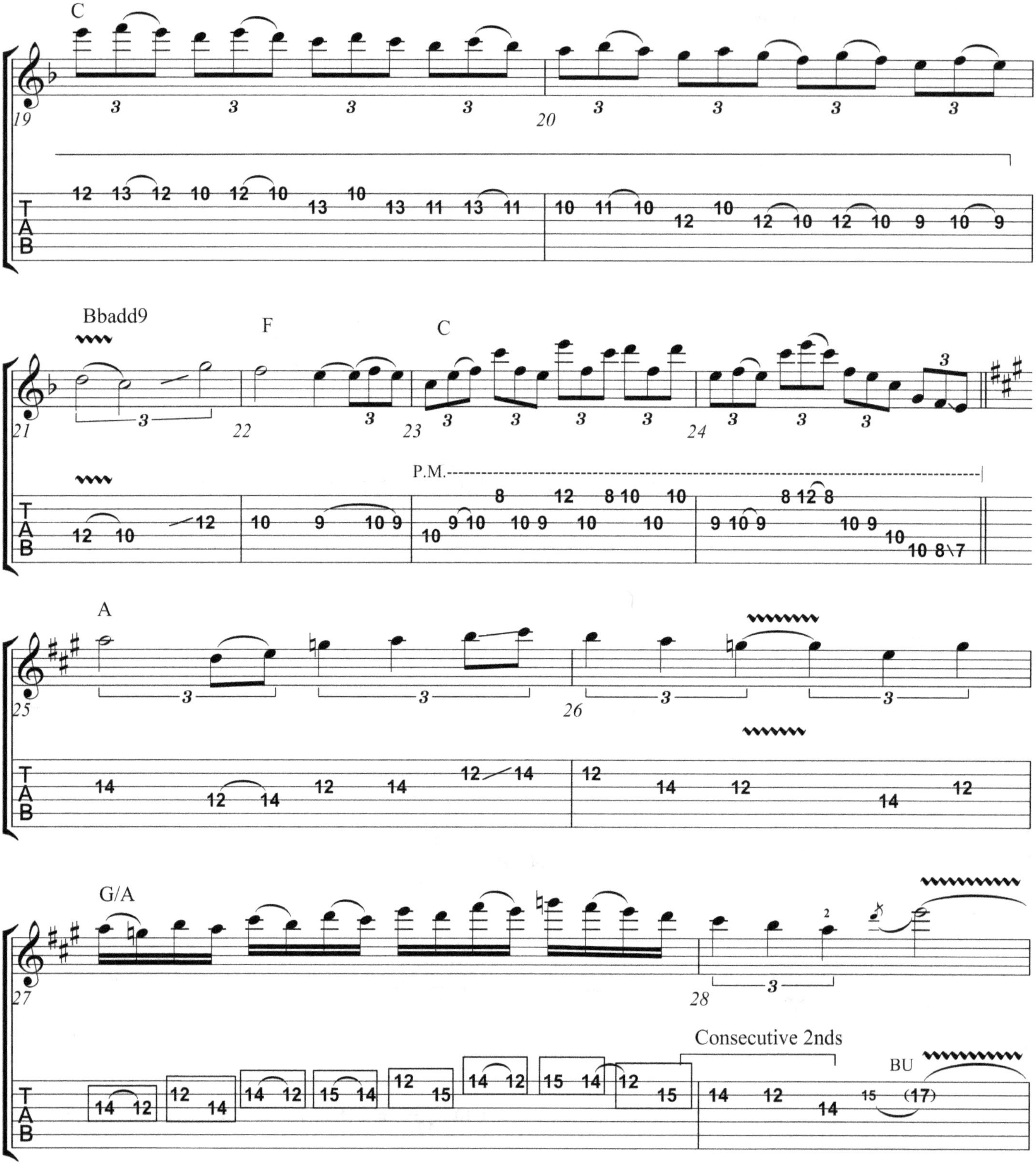
C
Bbadd9
F
C
P.M.
A
G/A
Consecutive 2nds
BU

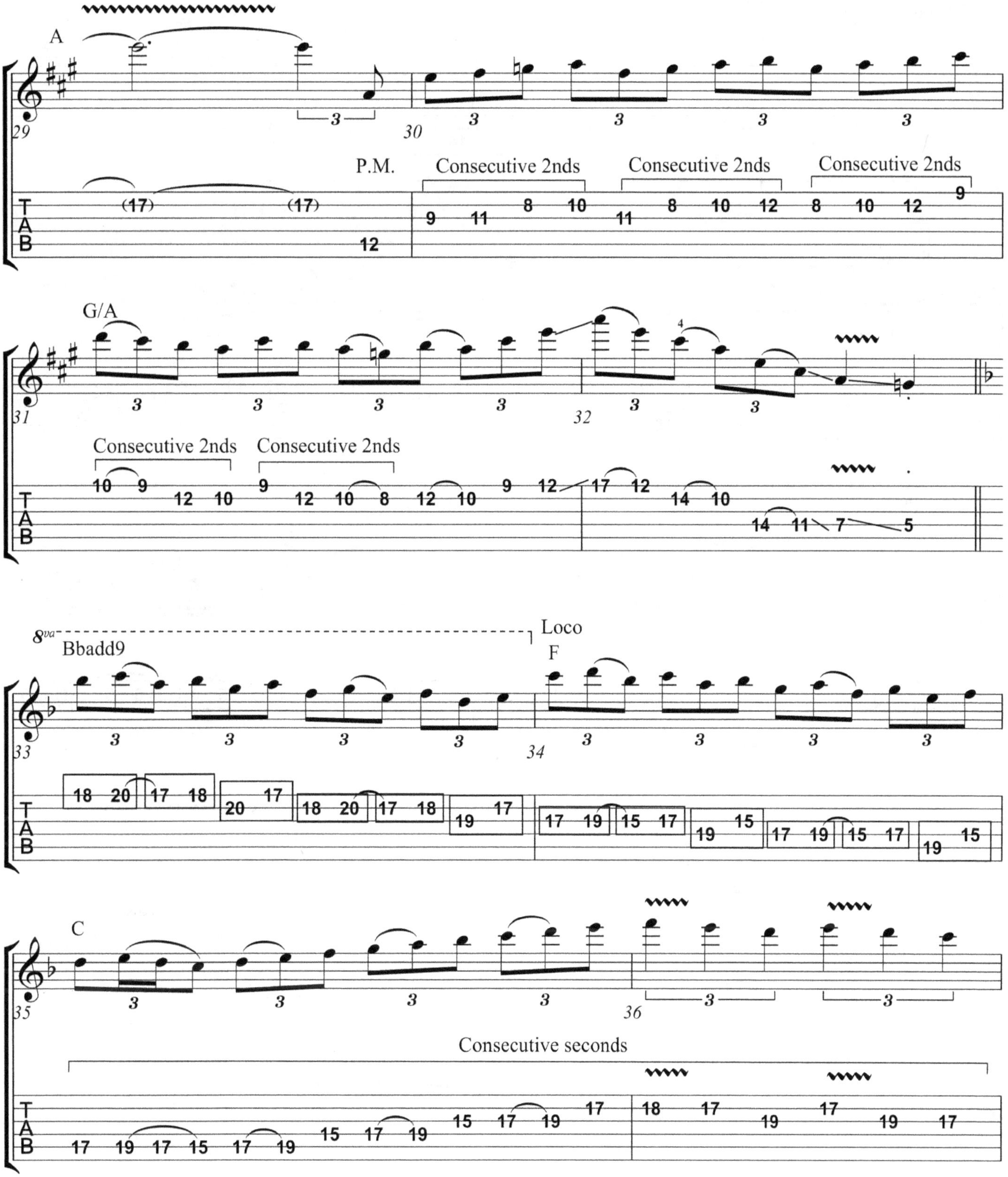
A
P.M.
Consecutive 2nds
Consecutive 2nds
Consecutive 2nds
G/A
Consecutive 2nds
Consecutive 2nds
8va
Bbadd9
Loco
F
C
Consecutive seconds

Bbadd9
F
BU
C
8va
BU
R
Loco
Bbadd9
(8)
F
C
Consecutive seconds
W. bar scoop
decay
Bbadd9
F
W. bar scoop
Consecutive seconds
Consecutive seconds

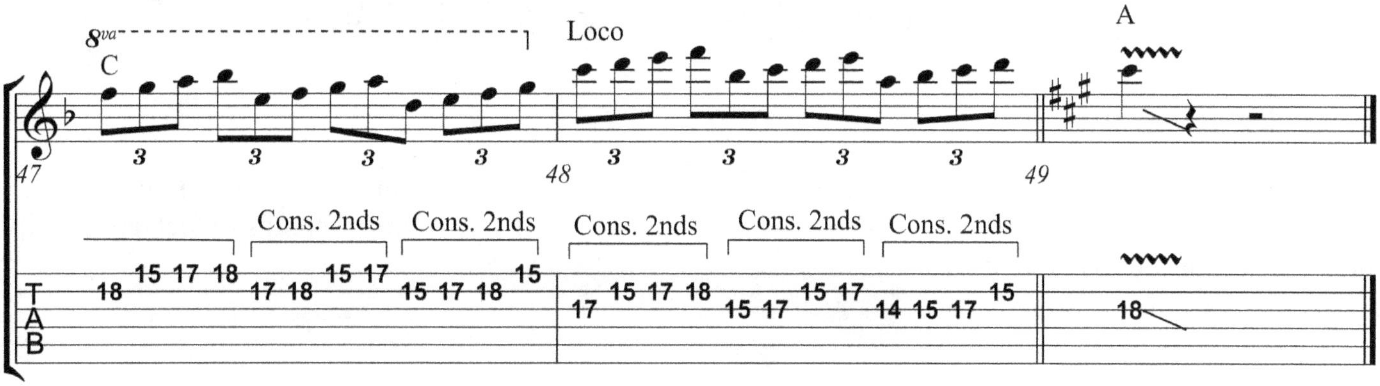
8va
C
Loco
A
47
48
49
Cons. 2nds
Cons. 2nds
Cons. 2nds
Cons. 2nds
Cons. 2nds
18 15 17 18 17 18 15 17 15 17 18 15
17 15 17 18 15 17 15 17 14 15 17 15
18

Chapter Two: Third Intervals Solo Study

Musical Effect

By playing every other note in the scale (diatonic thirds) our melodic ideas immediately sound richer, sweeter and more harmonically defined. This is because our single lines will start to imply chords (which are usually built by stacking consecutive thirds).

Technical Considerations

The transition from scale steps to melodic leaps in our solos allows us to use techniques like *tapping* (when consecutive thirds are played on a single string) and *sweep picking* (when consecutive thirds are played one-note-per-string). These can sometimes be challenging to perform accurately and require a certain level of technical proficiency.

Visualisation

To play thirds in the scale, you simply play every other note.

You can play one third (e.g., A – C), two consecutive thirds (e.g., A – C – E), three consecutive thirds (e.g., A – C – E –G) or more.

The following table shows what harmonic entities are created by playing consecutive thirds in A Mixolydian.

CONSECUTIVE THIRD COMBINATIONS		
Triads (3 note)	**Arpeggios (4 notes)**	**Super/Extended Arpeggios**
(Two consecutive third intervals)	(Three consecutive third intervals)	(Four or more consecutive third intervals)
A, C#, E = **A**	A, C#, E, G = **A7**	Example:
B, D, F# = **Bm**	B, D, F#, A = **Bm7**	A, C#, E, G, B, D = **A11**
C#, E, G = **C#o**	C#, E, G, B = **C#m7b5**	
D, F#, A = **D**	D, F#, A, C# = **Dmaj7**	
E, G, B = **Em**	E, G, B, D = **Em7**	
F#, A, C# = **F#m**	F#, A, C#, E = **F#m7**	
G, B, D = **G**	G, B, D, F# = **Gmaj7**	

Thankfully, playing third intervals when improvising isn't this cerebral – you can simply just play every other note in a scale!

Solo Performance Notes

While it's possible to identify every triad and arpeggio created by stacking thirds in this solo study, it's fine to simply think in terms of stacking thirds in the scale. The more intuitively you can use a concept, the better.

In the transcription, rectangular boxes around notes indicate the following:

- Rectangle around two notes = a single diatonic third interval

- Rectangle around three or more notes = multiple consecutive diatonic third intervals

Bars 1-6

Bars 3-4 contain a series of descending four-note arpeggios that ascend the scale. As these four-note groupings are played in triplets, each arpeggio becomes rhythmically displaced. A similar "4 against 3" effect is used in bars 14 and 37-38.

Bars 7-8

Lateral motion (moving along the length of the guitar string) often yields more expressive phrases because, in a relatively short distance, you are able to add a range of articulations (hammer-ons, pull-offs, bends, slides, vibrato etc) that are often left out when moving vertically in the same area of the neck. Here, we add expression by using a slide in between each three-note motif. A similar approach is taken in bars 27 and 31-32.

Bars 11-12

This passage is a series of two-octave diatonic arpeggios (up one, down the next) taken up through the scale in a "castle wall" pattern approach.

I played this on the recording using continuous sweeps of the picking hand and only using hammer-ons or pull-offs where there was more than one note on each string. This approach was also used in bars 28 and 34-36.

Bars 14-16

These three bars are entirely composed from Van Halen-style tapped one-string arpeggios.

Bar 14 contains more rhythmic displacement as the four-note groupings are played in a triplet count. Bars 15 and 16 each contain nested tuplets (in this case, 1/8th note triplets played in a 1/4 note triplet rhythm).

Bars 19-20

In bar 19 I take a series of ascending four-note arpeggios up through the scale and this is one of the very few times where I don't use economy picking (the act of travelling directly to each new string with the pick) in this solo. Bar 20 contains a mix of three-note triads and four-note arpeggios.

Bar 24

The final five notes of this bar form a C major triadic arpeggio that can be seen as stacked thirds in a 2 + 3 note-combination.

Bar 25

Thirds don't have to be played individually and this bar contains some rocky double-stops composed of stacked thirds.

Bars 26-29

In bar 28, each six-note arpeggio is built from stacked thirds. The same principle is also used in bar 30.

Bars 33-34

Aside from the final two notes, this passage explores the same nine-note super arpeggio shape.

Bars 35-36

Here I play a series of consecutive six-note motifs that are shifted down the guitar neck within the scale (starting with a two-note pick-up at the end of bar 34).

The open E string at the end of bar 36 is a filler allowing us to make the large position shift into the following bar.

Bars 41-46

This section features a combination of sweeps and legato playing, along with some right- and left-hand taps.

The 1-2-1-1-1-3 note-configuration of the nine-note arpeggio in bar 41 is shifted diatonically up through the scale. Each one is essentially a five-note and four-note arpeggio stacked on top of each other.

I use left-hand tapping when I descend each arpeggio, so each bar has just one down-sweep at the start. However, you can also use an up-sweep to descend in the second half if you prefer.

When deciding on which techniques to apply, remember that the listener should not be aware of the ones you are using. In this case, they should just hear a smooth, even stream of clear notes. It certainly shouldn't sound "sweepy".

Bars 47-48

We conclude with an ascending three-note sequence played in another nine-note super arpeggio.

TRI-UMPH

(Solo Study Featuring Third Intervals)

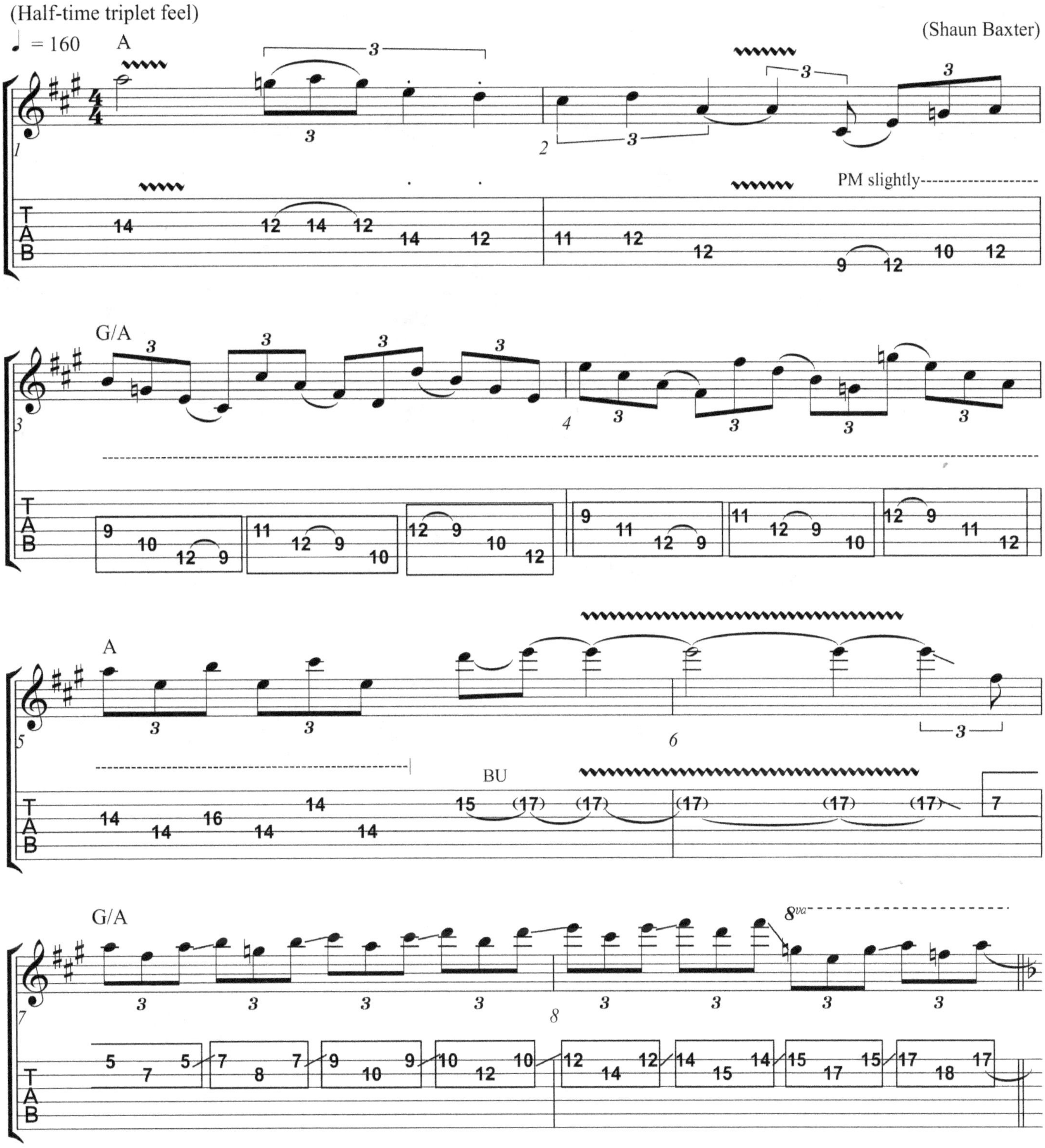

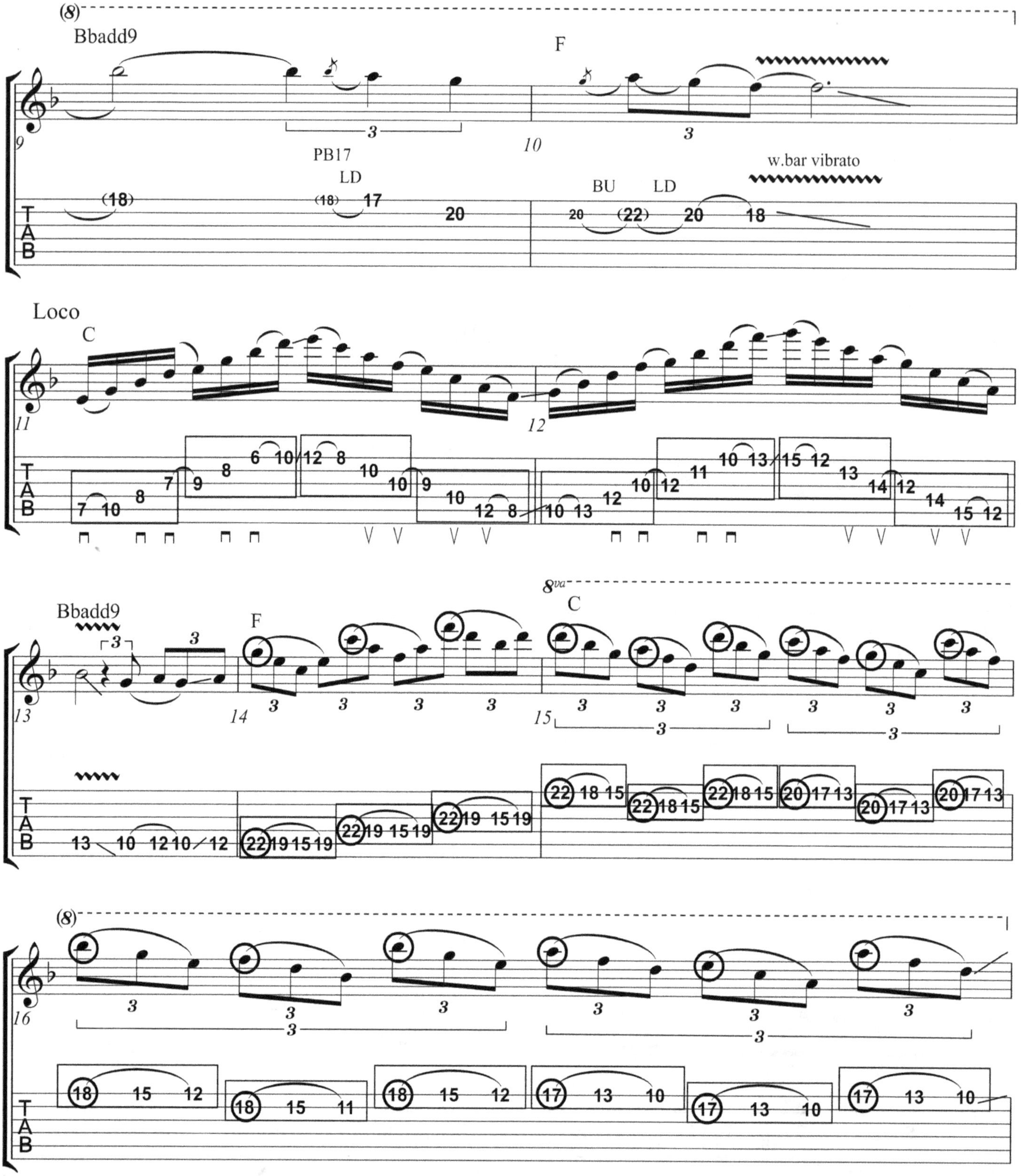
(8)
Bbadd9
F
PB17
LD
BU
LD
w.bar vibrato
Loco
C
Bbadd9
F
8va
C
(8)

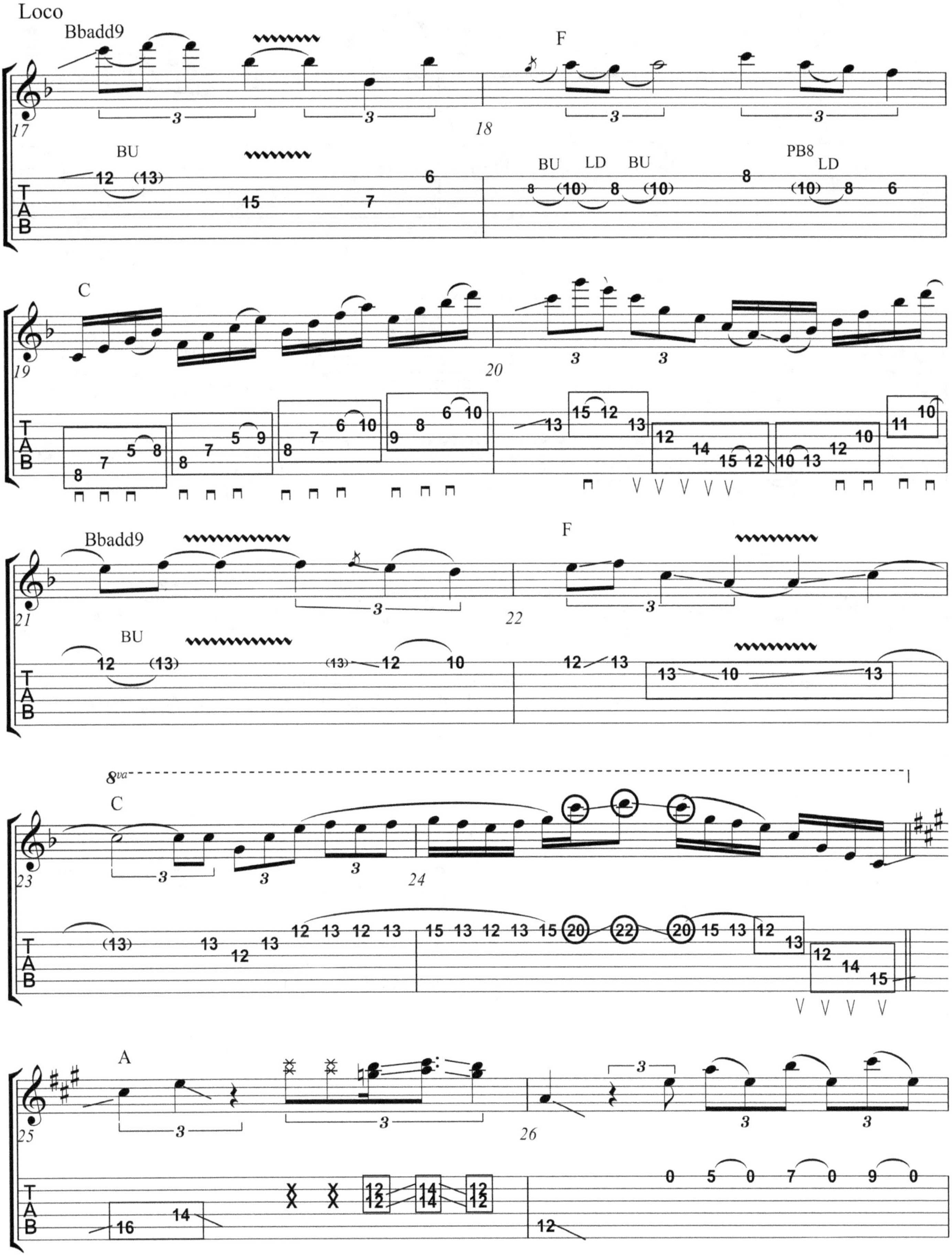
Loco
Bbadd9
F
BU
LD
PB8
C
8va
A

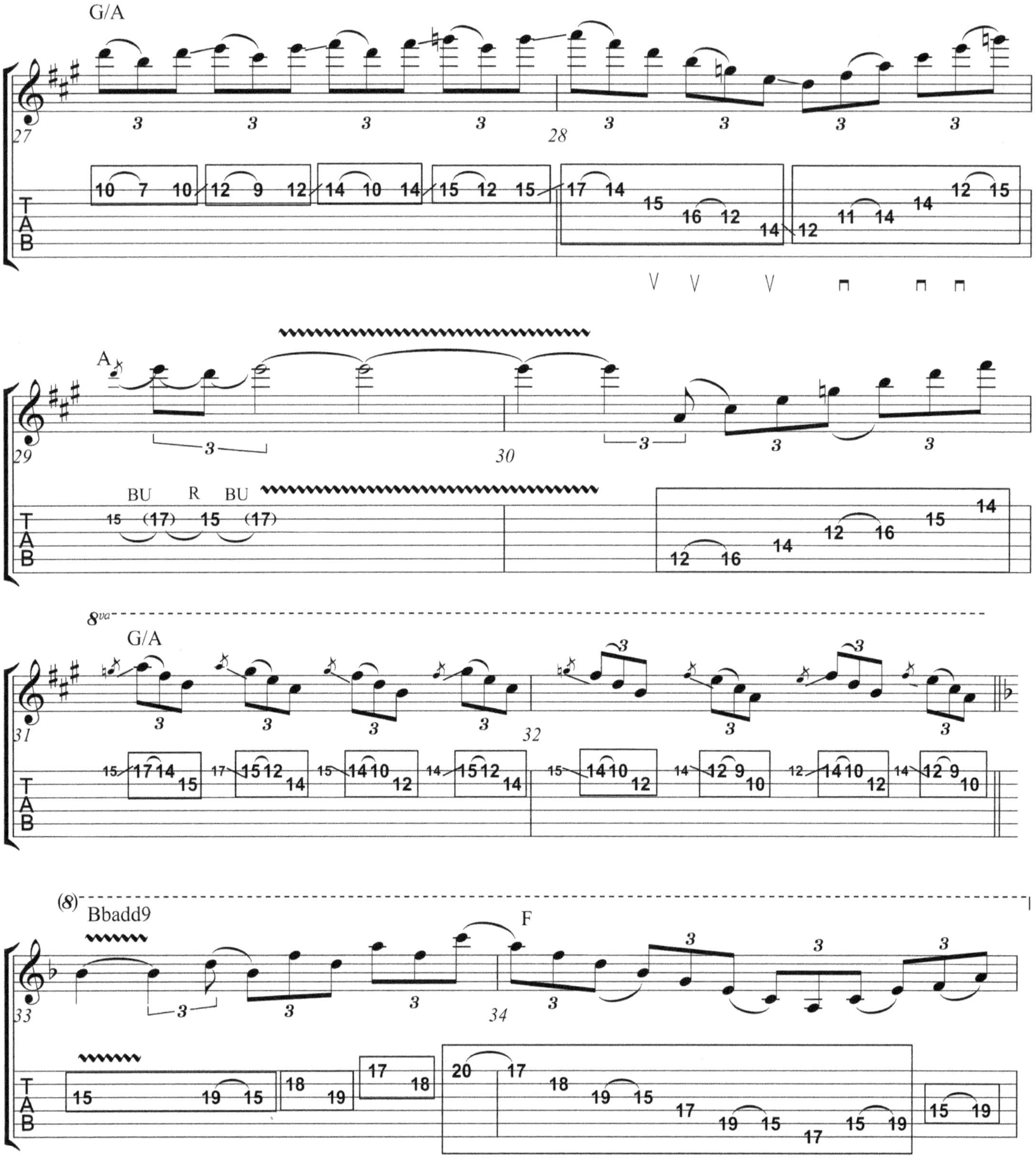
G/A
A
BU
R
BU
8va
G/A
(8)
Bbadd9
F

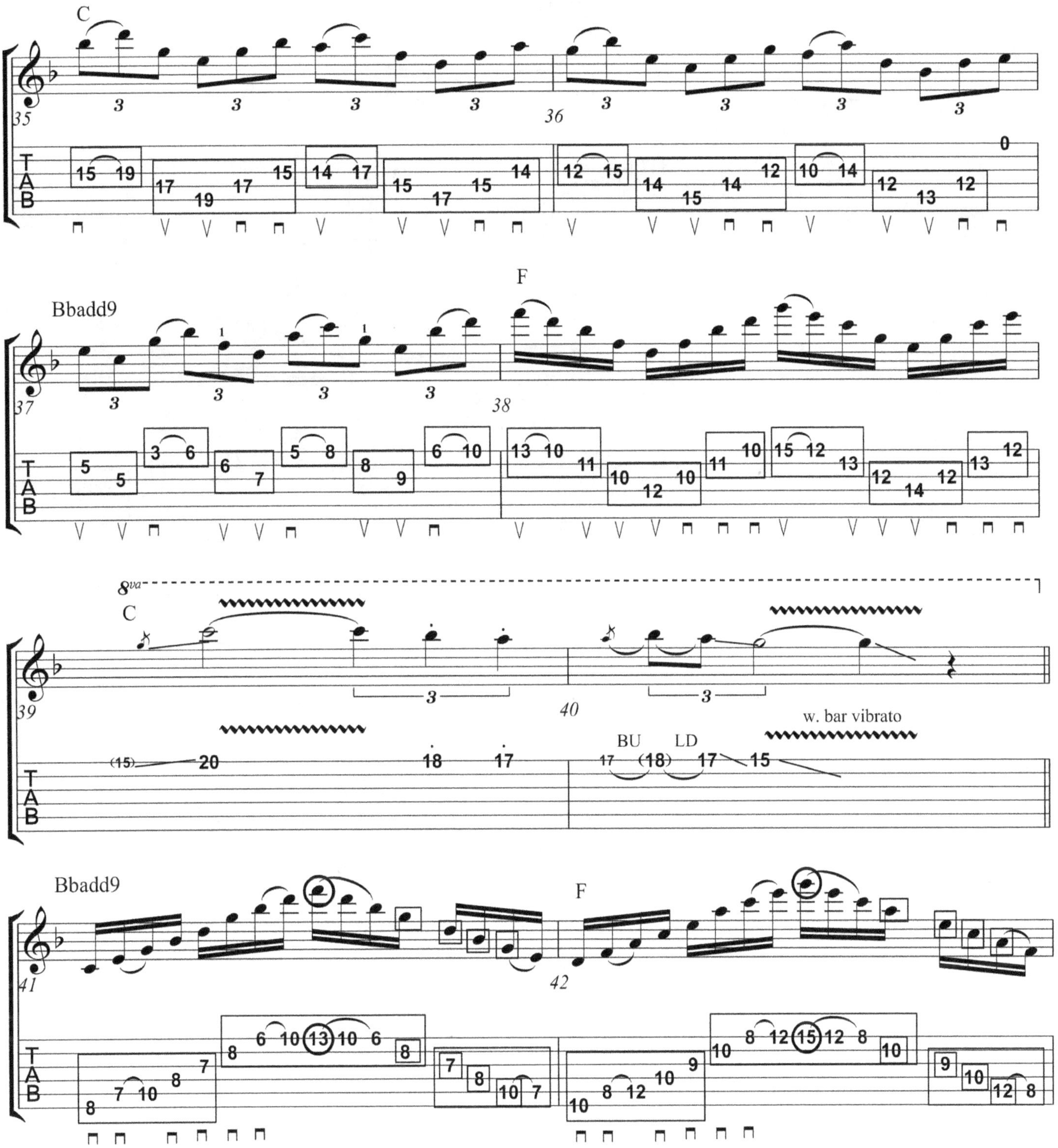
C
Bbadd9
F
8va
C
BU
LD
w. bar vibrato
Bbadd9
F

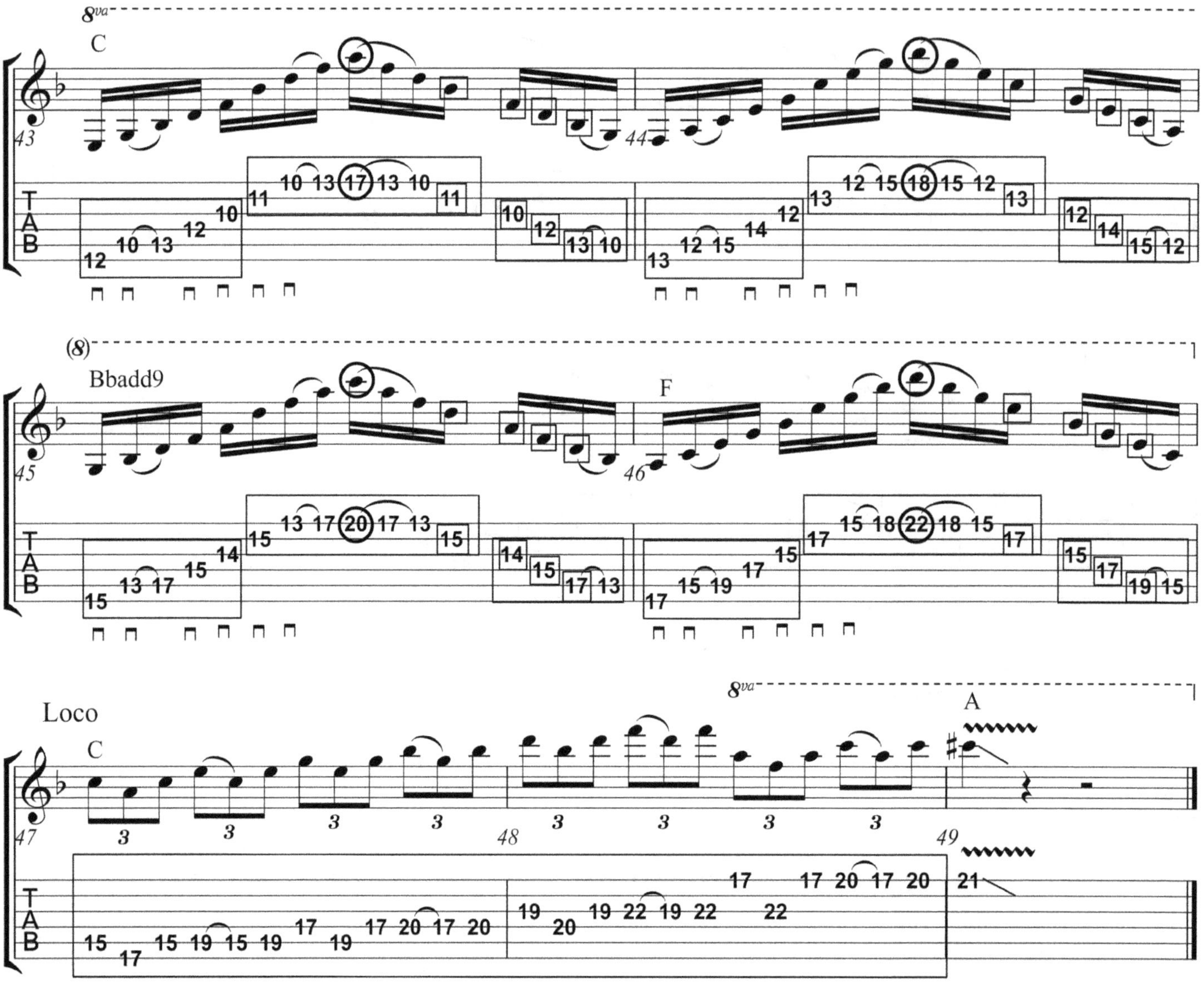
8va
C
(8)
Bbadd9
F
Loco
C
A

Chapter Three: Fourth Intervals Solo Study

Musical Effect:

Perfect fourths create an open, modern sound that is hard, angular, but also harmonically neutral. The waveforms created by fourths, fifths and octaves are more stable and less dissonant than other intervals when used with distortion, which means that fourths work well when played as double-stops. In fact, they form the basis of many classic rock riffs, such as *Smoke on the Water, Burn*, and *All Night Long* by Ritchie Blackmore.

Technical Considerations

Consecutive fourths are a technical challenge to perform. They can be stacked one-note-per-string and this requires barré rolls and/or palm muting to get enough separation between the notes.

Example 3a

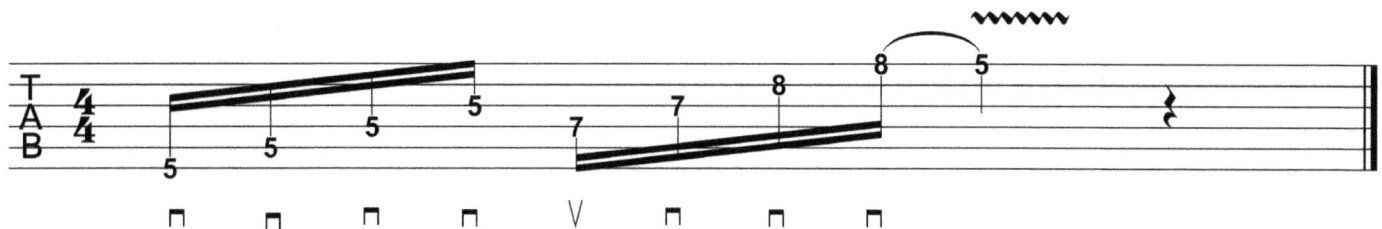

A **barré roll** is a technique used to play consecutive notes on different strings at the same fret. One finger of the fretting hand is laid across two or more strings and the pressure of the fingerprint pad (or the underside of the finger if there are many strings) is rolled from string to string, so that only one note is held down at any one time while the others are gently muted. This movement is created with an arm and wrist action rather than altering the shape of the finger, which should remain quite straight but slightly arched throughout.

Using the barré roll when moving from a thicker string to a thinner one is relatively straightforward, as you play the first note on the thicker string with the tip of the finger, then play the next note on the thinner string with the fingerprint part of the same finger.

Using the technique when moving from a thinner string to a thicker one, however, requires a bit more forethought, as it involves playing the first note on the thinner string with the fingerprint part of the finger, so there is enough fingertip left to roll onto the next note on the thicker string.

Some fusion players, like Allan Holdsworth and Scott Henderson, prefer to play perfect fourth intervals on the same string, even though the stretch is quite wide. Here is the same line played with wide stretches, hammer-ons and string skips.

Example 3b

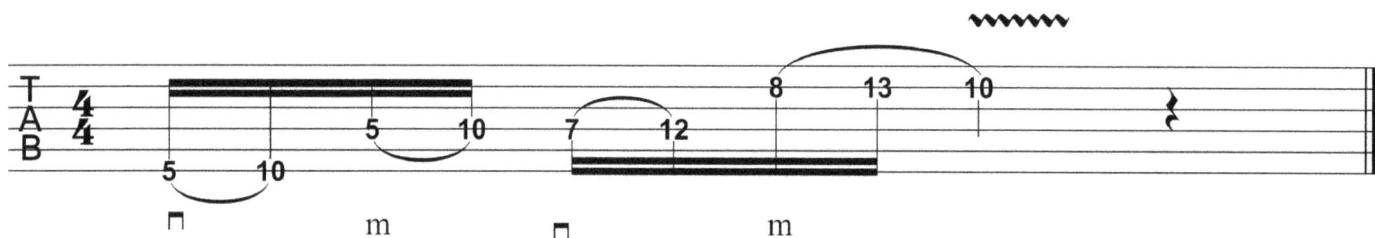

It is actually possible to play five consecutive fourths on a single string if you use a large stretch, two right-hand taps and an open string.

Five Notes on One String (Consecutive Fourths)

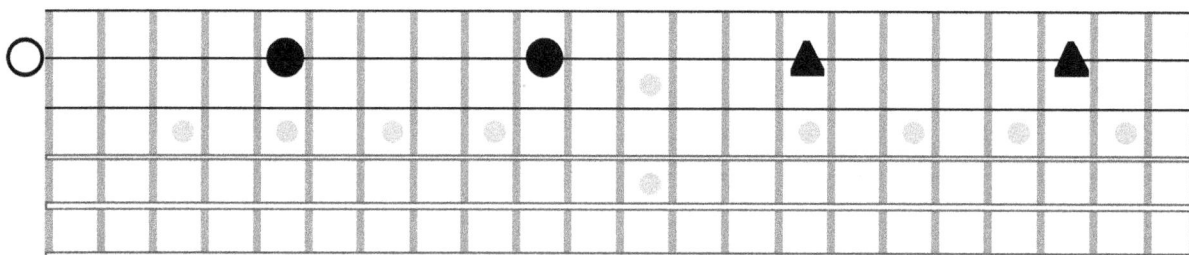

Whichever way you play these fourths, it's good to look for straight lines across the neck because they are easy to see and play. You can see these symmetrical forms in A Mixolydian below. Many of these feature in the following solo study, either as written, or transposed to C Mixolydian.

Straight Lines Using Fourth Intervals in A Mixolydian

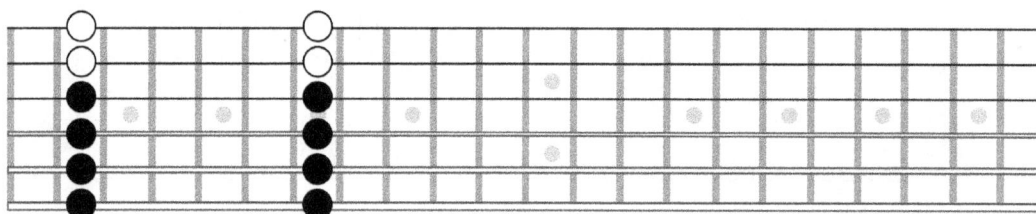

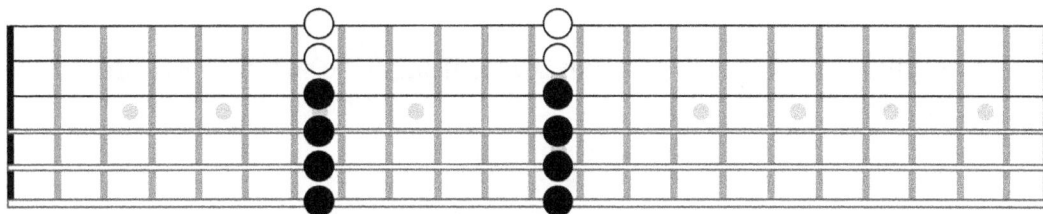

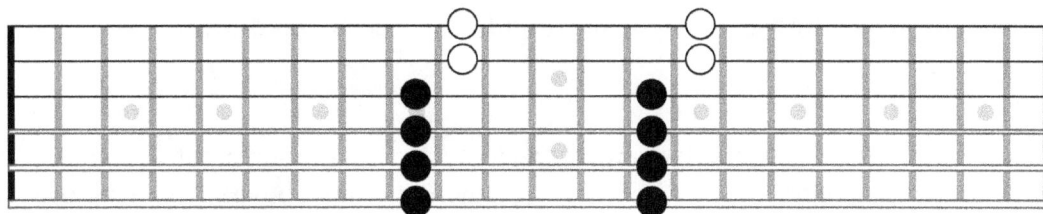

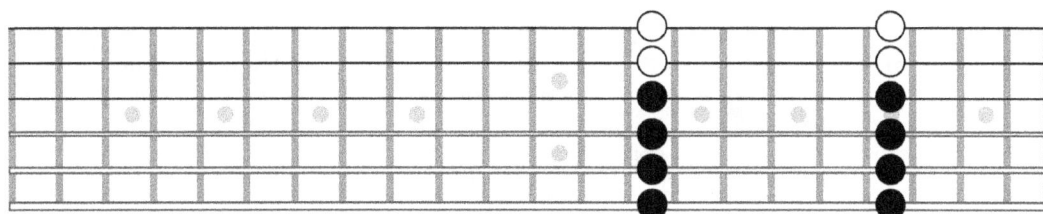

Solo Performance Notes

- In the transcription, rectangular boxes around notes indicate the following:

- Rectangle around two notes = a single diatonic fourth interval

- Rectangle around three or more notes = multiple consecutive diatonic fourth intervals

Bars 1-2

We start with a series of motifs built from stacked fourths on a single string using a combination of left- and right-hand tapping – an approach synonymous with Eddie Van Halen.

The idea in bar two requires that you switch between a left-hand finger and a right-hand tap to play the same note on the 14th fret which doubles the speed of a trill. You'll use this approach again in bar five.

Bars 3-4

This passage is divided into four-note sections and a "4 against 3" cross rhythm is created as you play these four-note groups in triplets. There are other examples of this 4:3 rhythm in bar 10 and bars 35-36.

Bar 6

These large six-note structures are built from consecutive fourths played using wide stretches and string skips. This approach is also used in bar 47.

Bar 7

Listen to how the angular effect of using fourths creates an interesting motif.

Bar 10

The four-note motifs in this bar are created by ascending up one fourth and descending the next.

Bars 15-16

Most of the fourths in major modes, including Mixolydian, are *perfect fourths* (a distance of five frets), so there are many opportunities to use symmetry on the fretboard (see the diagrams above). This idea uses a combination of wide stretches and string skips to avoid playing consecutive notes on different strings at the same fret.

Bars 17-18

Apart from the occasional tone-wide trill, the melody in this section is composed entirely of fourths.

Bars 21-22

The first seven notes of this section form a large ascending structure built by stacking consecutive fourths (the B natural is used as a grace-note to the C). The descending equivalent is used in bar 48.

Bars 23-24

This is almost a descending equivalent of the ascending symmetrical passage in bars 15-16.

I moved laterally here, playing bar 24 on the A, D and G strings rather than higher up the neck on the E, A and D strings. I did this to place the fretting hand in the right area to start the tapping section in bar 25.

Bars 25-30

This section is a transcription of something that I improvised during the recording, which is why there are various odd-note groupings, such as the quintuplet in bar 30. They may look complicated, but these rhythmic variations are natural and well-balanced. They have a better flow and sound less rigid.

Bar 25 is the first example of nested tuplets (here, 1/8th note triplets and 1/16th notes are played over a 1/4 note triplet pulse). There are more examples of this in bars 27-30 and 41-42.

The second half of bar 29 uses a left-hand tap with the first finger to play the first note on each string. The right-hand taps actually make this easier, although it is vital to practice the specific sequence of movements that allow you to play a passage like this with strength and accuracy.

Combining Left- & Right-Hand Taps When Ascending a Scale or Arpeggio

1) The second right-hand tap in bar 29 makes it possible for the fretting hand to leave the fretboard so that it can play the following left-hand tap (9th fret of the A string) from sufficient height to get a strong note.

2) When the left-hand tap is played, it is important that the previous right-hand tap does not spring up in an exchange, as this will create open-string noise. Instead, soften the pressure on the right-hand tapped note but do not remove contact from the string. This takes the vibrating energy out of the string and allows the finger to finally lift without unwanted noise.

3) Leave the string gently and in such a way that you simultaneously dampen it with the side of the picking hand.

4) This sequence is repeated on all three occasions that the same movement occurs during the last nine notes of this bar.

This precise sequence of movements needs to be programmed slowly before it is sped up. Once you have mastered it, it should be used every time you encounter this same idea.

Bars 31-32

While most of the previous tapping sections were led with a right-hand tap on the downbeat, here a left-hand tap takes the lead, which creates a less predictable effect. This approach is also used in bars 41-42.

Bar 34

More fourths motifs here. The open string at the end of bar 34 buys time for the fretting hand to get ready for bar 35.

Bars 37-40

We couldn't explore fourths without some double-stops as they are so integral to the history of rock guitar.

Bar 43

Here, because of the standard guitar tuning, the symmetrical pattern of fourths changes as we move onto the second and first strings.

Bars 45-49

Bars 45 and 46 show stacked fourths where each note is played on a different string, creating vertical forms that have to be played with **barré rolls**. Bar 47 uses an alternative approach that requires wide stretches, string skips and legato technique which, although it produces more sonic clarity, requires accuracy across a wide area of the neck and can feel a bit more difficult. We finish with a brazen descent of stacked fourths, one played on each string, to give you a true and distinctive flavour of this interesting interval.

FAB FOUR

(Solo Study Featuring Fourth Intervals)

(Half-time triplet feel)

(Shaun Baxter)

8va
F
C
(8)
Bbadd9
Loco
F
BU
PB15
LD
C
Consecutive 4ths
Consecutive 4ths
Consecutive 4ths
Consecutive 4ths
Bbadd9
F
C
Bbadd9
F
Consecutive 4ths
BU

C
Consecutive 4ths
Consecutive 4ths
Consecutive 4ths
Consecutive 4ths
A
G/A
A

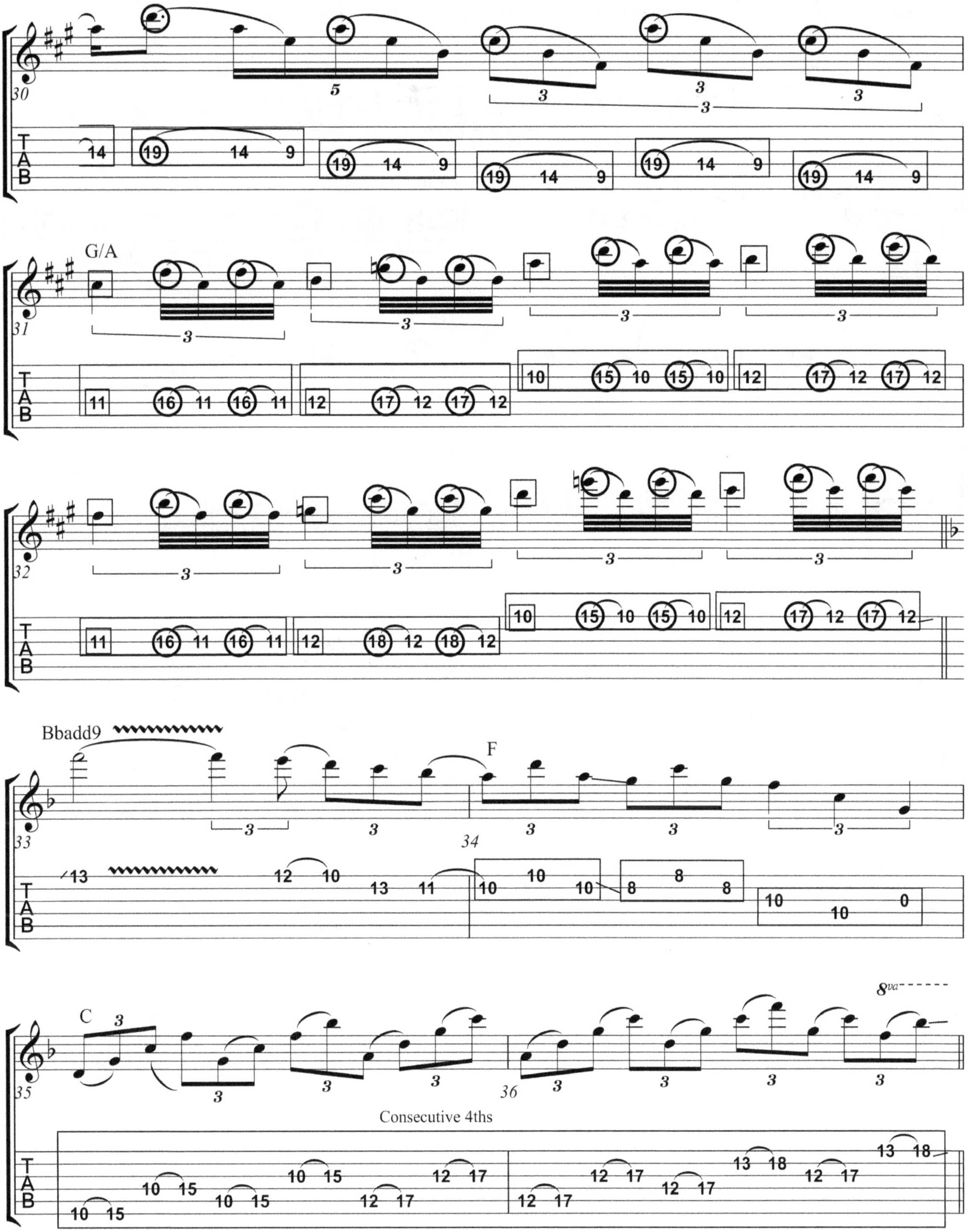
G/A
Bbadd9
F
C
Consecutive 4ths
8va

(8)
Bbadd9
F
C
Loco
4th Doublestops
Bbadd9
F
m
C
Bbadd9
F
Consec. 4ths
Consec. 4ths
Consec. 4ths
Consec. 4ths
Consec. 4ths
Consec. 4ths

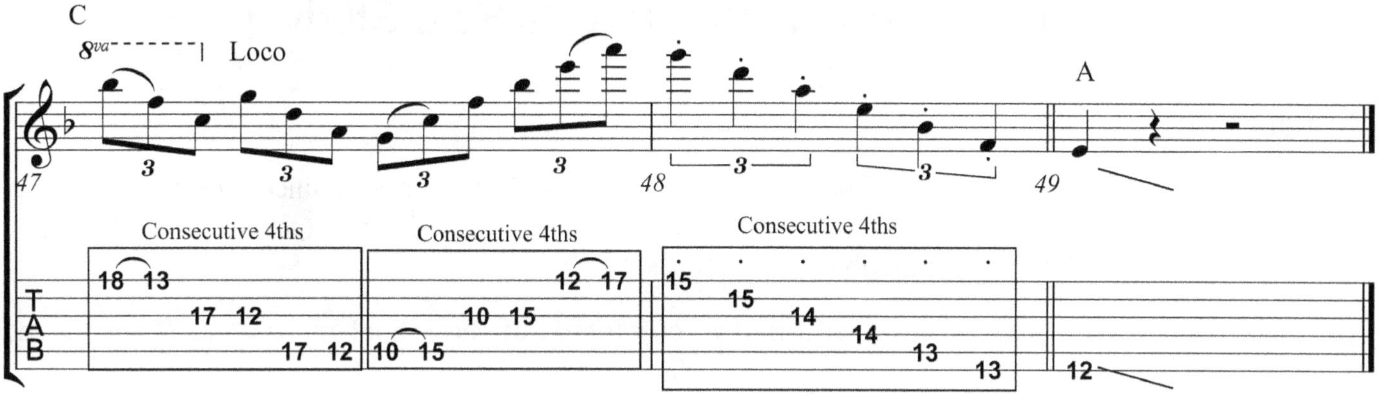
C
8va
Loco
A
47
48
49
Consecutive 4ths
Consecutive 4ths
Consecutive 4ths
T
A
B

Chapter Four: Fifth Intervals Solo Study

Musical Effect:

Perfect fifths sound open, angular and modern, and are in fact similar to fourths, since a perfect fifth is an inverted perfect fourth. For example, ascending from C to G is a perfect fifth interval (seven semitones), while descending from C to G is a perfect fourth (five semitones).

Fifths feature in many famous heavy metal riffs by Tony Iommi of Black Sabbath, such as *Paranoid* and *Heaven and Hell*.

Technical Considerations

Playing consecutive fifths using just the fretting hand on a single string becomes almost impossible below the 12th fret due to the large stretches required. However, when consecutive fifths are laid out on adjacent strings, they assume a convenient step configuration that is quite easy to play with a left-hand tap on each string.

Stacked Fifth Intervals

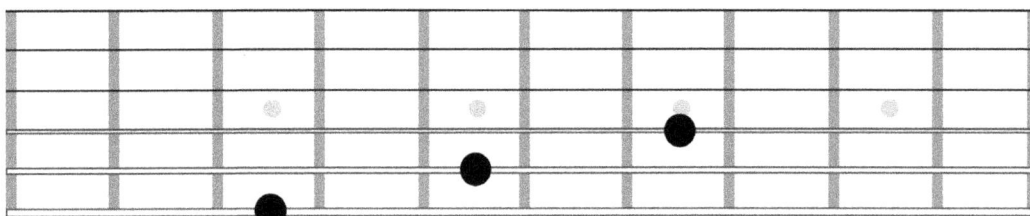

As usual, in the transcription you'll see that some notes have rectangular boxes around them.

- Rectangle around two notes = a single diatonic fifth interval

- Rectangle around three or more notes = multiple consecutive diatonic fifth intervals

Solo Performance Notes

In the transcription of our solo study, *Full Hand*, you will see a lot of left-hand tapping as this approach takes the pressure off the picking hand, and the resulting tone sounds fatter and more three-dimensional than using a pick for every note.

You'll also see that some passages require more than one finger of the picking hand to tap. Although it is possible to tap using the 2nd and 3rd fingers while holding the pick, the movement will be stronger if you dispense with the pick (perhaps holding it in your mouth) and tap with your first finger.

Listen carefully to the audio and try to hear which pickup I used. The opening passage uses the neck pickup for a warm, fluid sound. It would not sound the same if played using the bridge pickup.

Bars 0-3

We begin with an example of the stacked shapes shown above. Throughout the solo, you will see many shapes built from either two- or three- note units played on adjacent strings to form step shapes like this in the same line.

Pay attention to the pull-off between the third and fourth notes of each six-note motif. These make life easier for the picking hand and contribute to the overall smoothness of the sound.

Bar 4

This bar alternates between ascending and descending two-note motifs and uses the bridge pickup with palm muting and pinched harmonics for a contrast in tone.

The left-hand tap at the end of this bar allows time for your picking hand to switch pickup for the following section.

Bars 5-6

It's back to the neck pickup here to play a symmetrical pattern on each string-pair.

In bar five, the consecutive four-note motifs become rhythmically displaced when played to a triplet count. The additional note after each three-note motif in bar 6 creates an effective "4 against 3" feel.

As we're playing every note in bar 5 with the fretting hand, the pull-offs make life easier on the picking hand. Pull-offs are great because we get to play a note even when leaving a string.

Bars 7-8

Here is a similar passage of consecutive two-note fifth shapes, this time combining left- and right-hand tapping. I used the neck pickup here as it was smoother and there wasn't enough time to change pickups.

Bars 9-10

Here, we're using C Major Pentatonic. As you can see there are fifth intervals in that too.

C Major Pentatonic Scale Shape 1

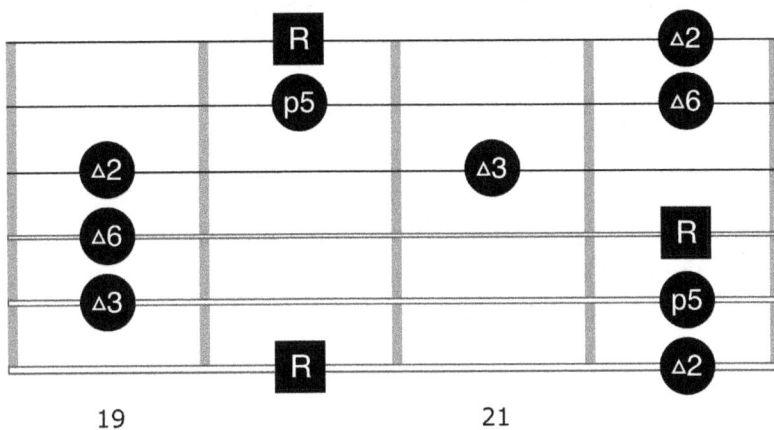

Bar 11

Next, we see a return of the forms used in bars 1-2 and a demonstration of a six-note ascending motif followed immediately by its descending equivalent.

Bar 12

This bar demonstrates how you can create four-note motifs from three-note shapes.

It's possible to finger each four-note cell in a different way. For example, the first two notes of the first motif could be left-hand tapped at the 12th and 10th frets of the D and A strings, and the final two could be right-hand tapped at the 17th and 19th frets of the A and D strings.

Bar 14

As in bar 7, this bar contains more two-note motifs played using a combination of left- and right-hand tapping only. This time, they alternate between ascending and descending and are played as triplets.

Bar 15

As we're high enough up the neck, it's possible to play fifth intervals on the same string with wide stretches rather than with a right-hand tap.

Bars 17-18

This Steve Vai style passage might sound like I've used a whammy pedal, but it's all quick fifth interval slides played with pinched harmonics.

Bar 19

This passage sounds smooth due to its combination of picked and tapped notes and is easier to play at speed than picking. In bar 19 pick only on the start of each beat. I added slight palm muting to give everything more punch and separation.

Bar 21

This bar features stacked fifths: one on each string pair (E-A, D-G, B-E).

Bars 23-32

Here's a different way of playing three-note motifs using a combination of strings skips with left- and right-hand tapping. As in bar 14, these four-note motifs played as triplets create a "4 against 3" feel.

Bar 32 rounds off this section with a variation on the approach used in bars 7 and 14.

Bars 33-36

These four bars contain four-note shapes created by adding a right-hand tap to the three-note shapes encountered in bar one. It's like a surgically enhanced version of the stacked three-note shapes made famous by Joe Satriani and originally used by modern jazz players like Joe Diorio and Don Mock.

Bars 41-46

These bars show the parallel relationship between a pair of two-note-per-string pentatonic shapes played a perfect fifth apart (in this case the D Minor and A Minor Pentatonic scales). Once again, you'll need to use a combination of left- and right-hand tapping reminiscent of eight-fingered tapper T. J. Helmerich.

F Major (Dm) Pentatonic scale and C (Am) Major Pentatonic Scale

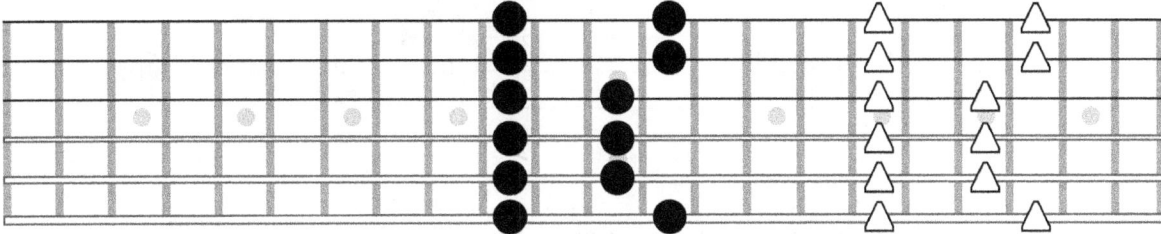

No rock study on fifth intervals would be complete without a *power chord* hence the F5 at the start of bar 46.

Bars 47-48

In the right keys, open strings can come in handy to play fifths as they are a fairly large interval.

The solo finishes off with an idea featuring open strings and ten-note groupings, which help to add fresh rhythmic interest.

FULL HAND
(Solo Study Featuring Fifth Intervals)

(Shaun Baxter)

(Half-time triplet feel)

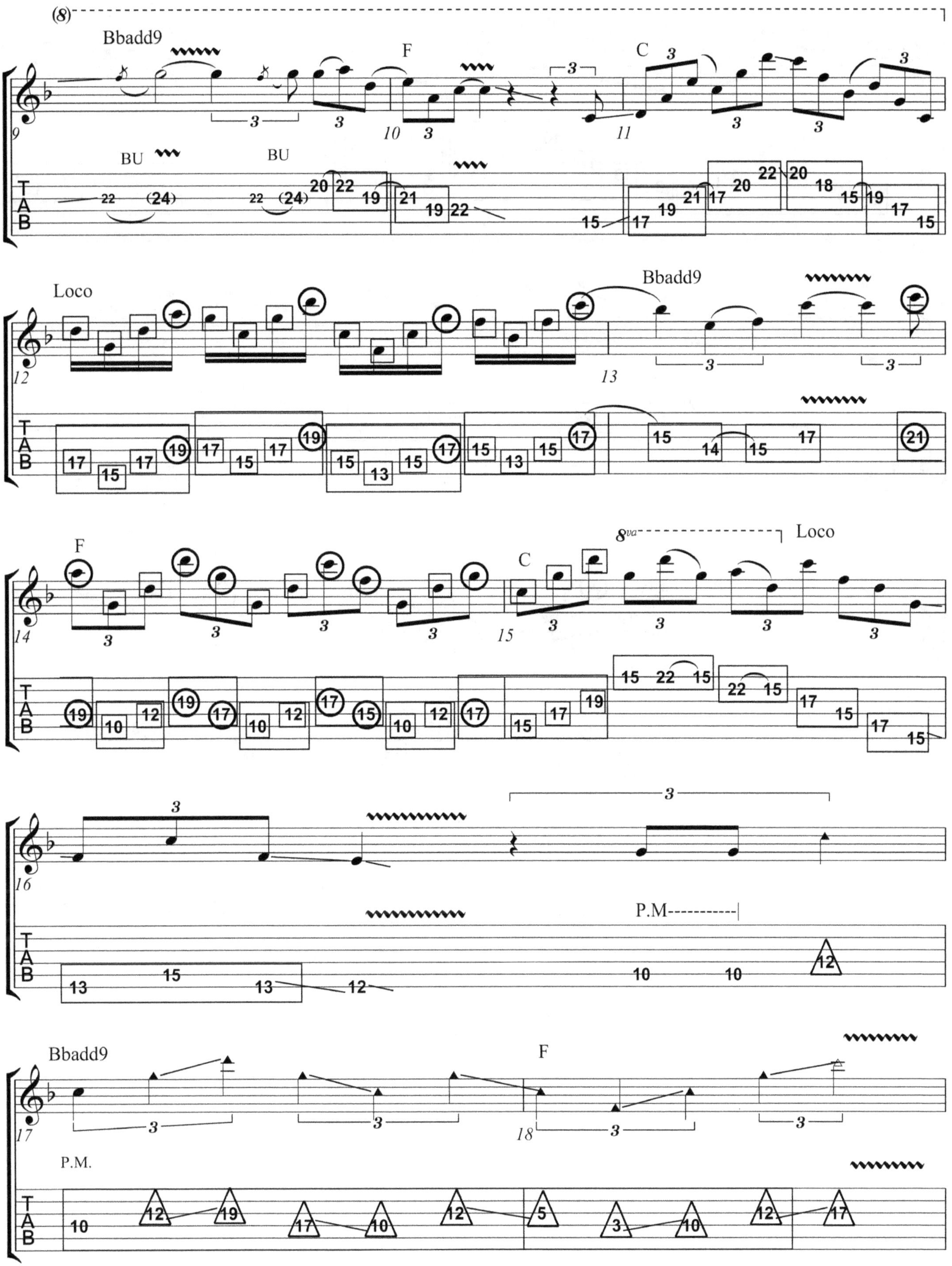
(8)
Bbadd9
F
C
BU
BU
Loco
Bbadd9
F
C
8va
Loco
P.M
Bbadd9
F
P.M.

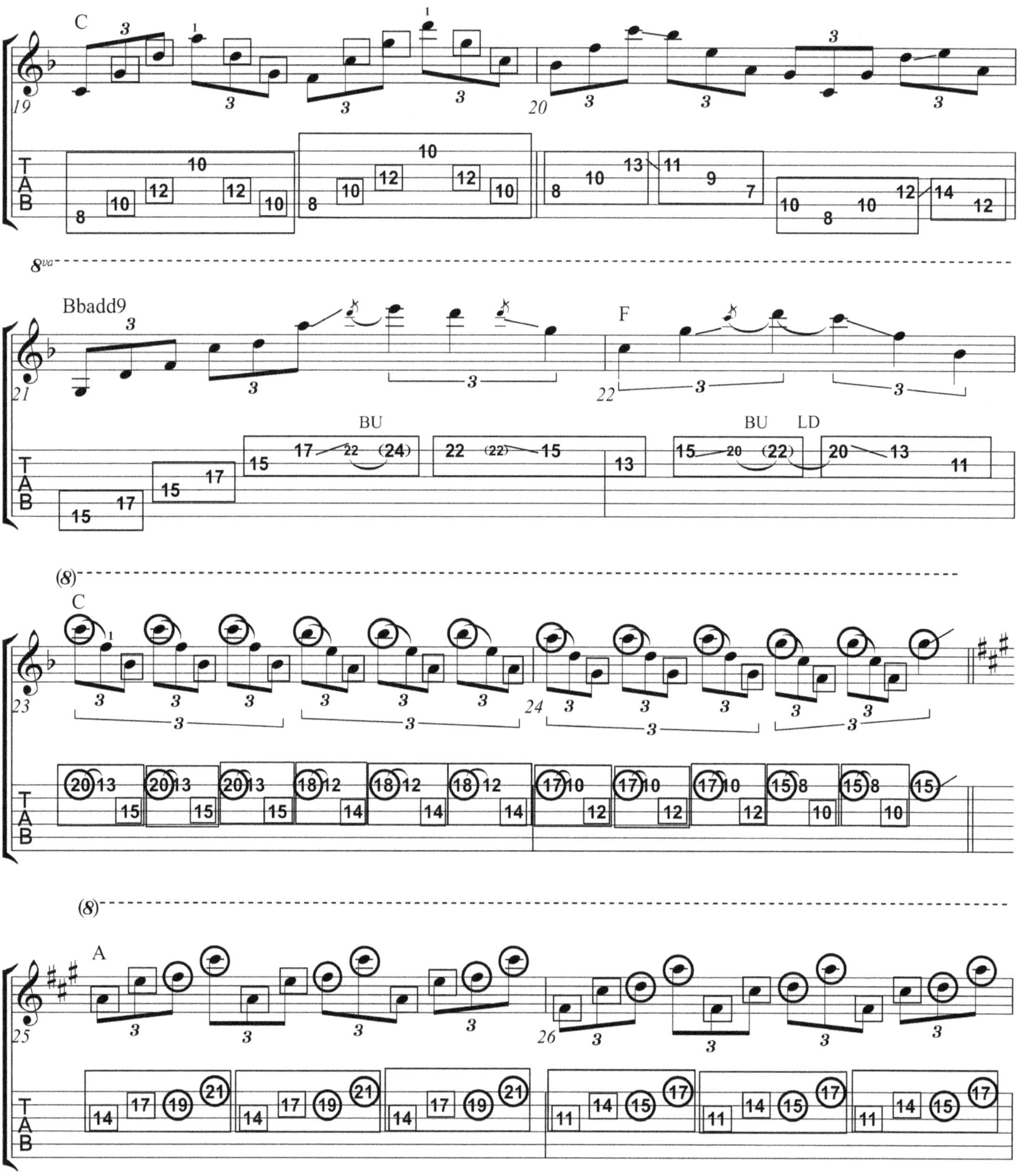
C
Bbadd9
F
C
A
8va
BU
LD
TAB

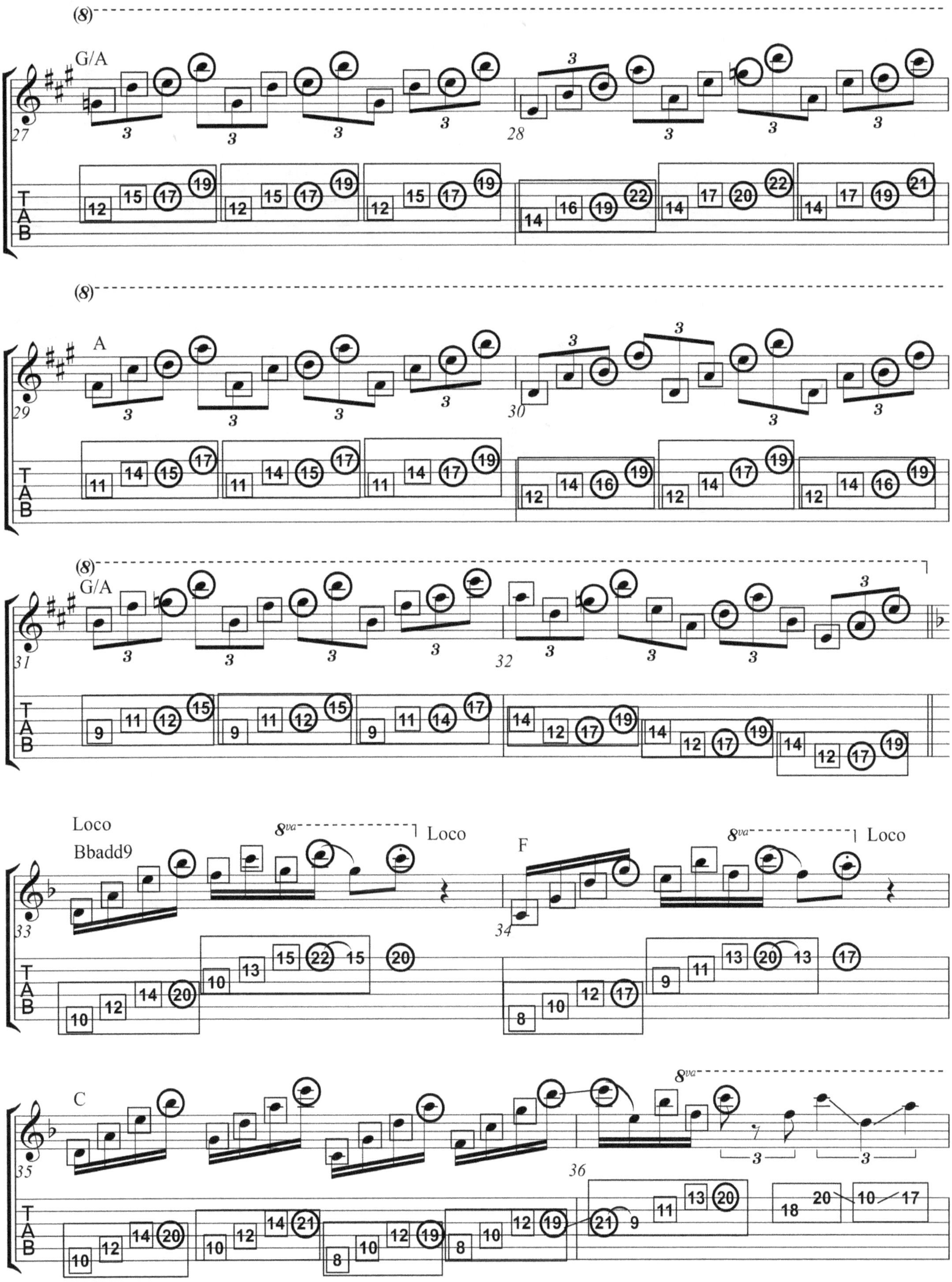
(8)
G/A
(8)
A
(8)
G/A
Loco
Bbadd9
8va
Loco
F
8va
Loco
C
8va

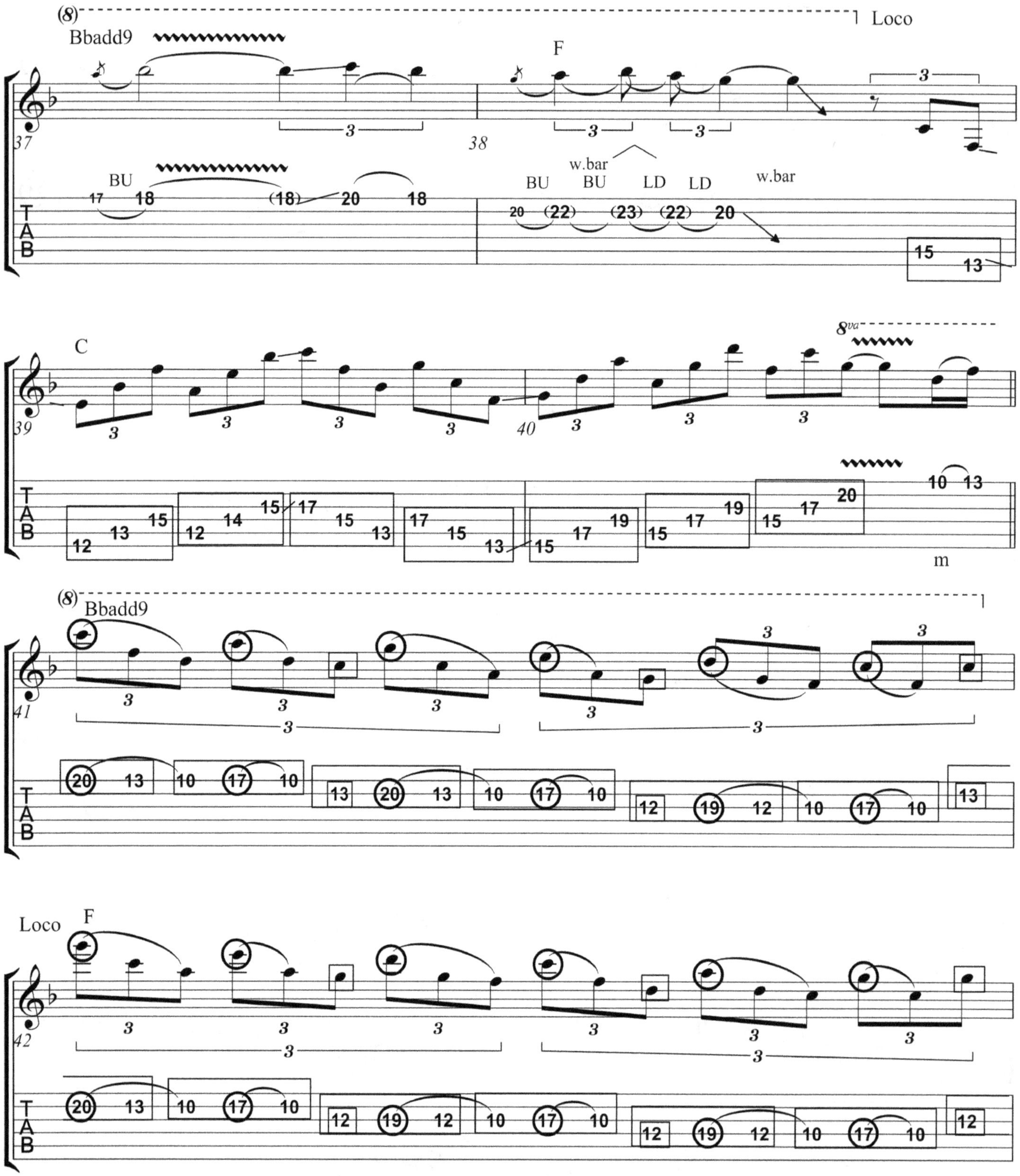
(8)
Loco
Bbadd9
F
BU
w.bar
BU
BU
LD
LD
w.bar
C
8va
m
(8)
Bbadd9
Loco
F

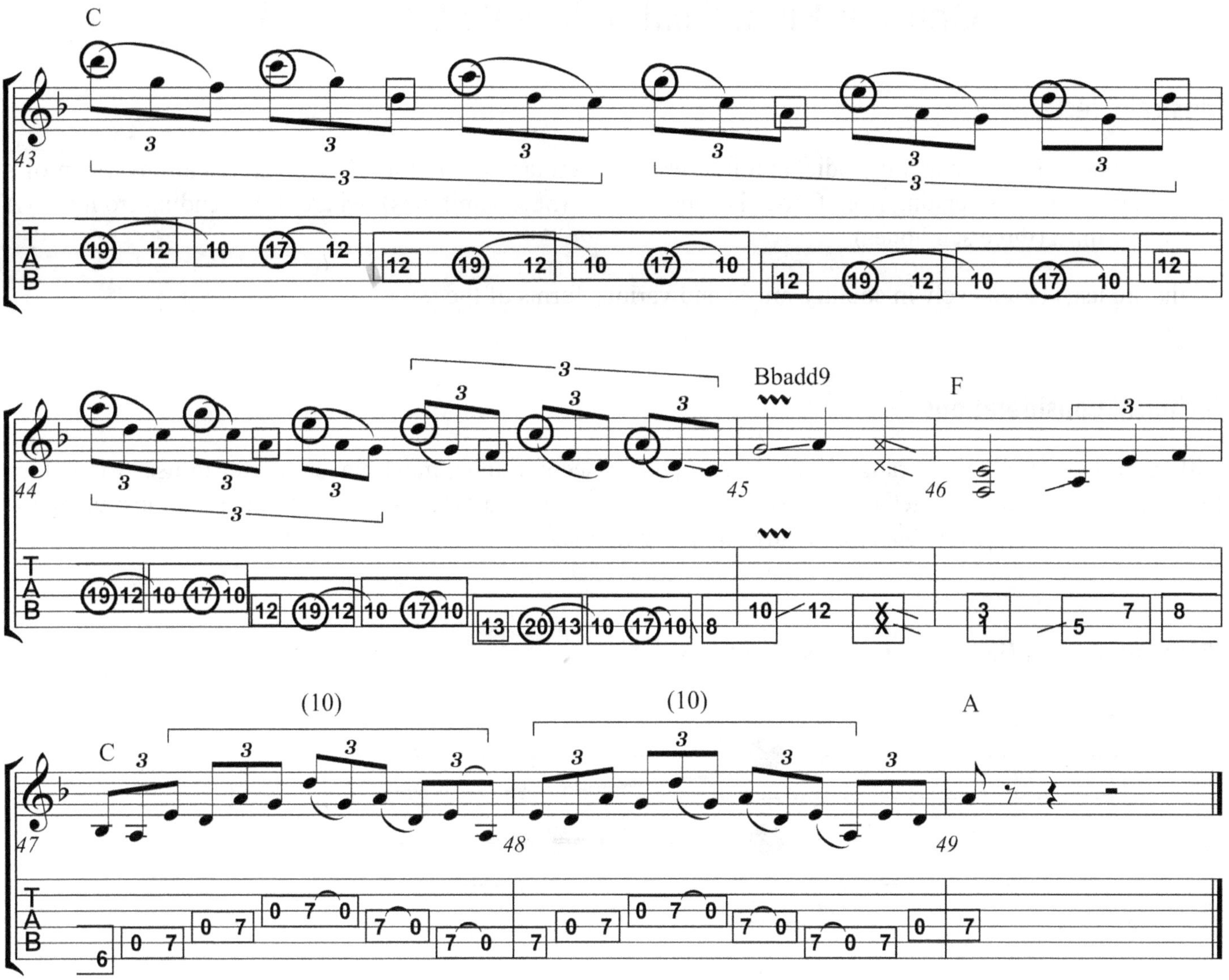
C
Bbadd9
F
C
(10)
(10)
A

Chapter Five: Sixth Intervals Solo Study

Musical Effect

Sixths sound soft, sweet and melodic, and in a way are similar to thirds. In fact, a sixth is an inversion of a third. For example, ascending from C to A is a major sixth (nine semitones), whereas descending from C to A is a minor third (three semitones).

Sixths are used extensively in country music and various forms of the blues.

Technical Considerations

Although it is possible to arrange sixth intervals on adjacent strings, most players prefer to use string skips to bring the notes closer together. This is where hybrid picking starts to make sense rather than just using the pick, and is a technique favoured by many country guitarists.

Sixth Interval: Adjacent String vs String Skip

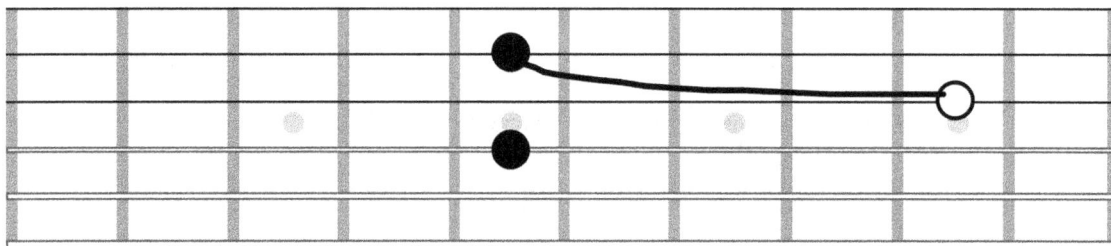

Solo Performance Notes

In the transcription you'll notice that some notes have rectangular boxes around them.

- Rectangle around two notes = a single diatonic sixth interval
- Rectangle around three or more notes = multiple consecutive diatonic sixth intervals

Throughout this solo, try to be aware of not just the interval type, but the distance between them, as various interval-based motifs trace pathways across the neck.

Bars 0-8

The opening section combines picking with left- and right-hand taps and is supported by a melody in the backing track that emphasises the high notes in the continuous stream of 1/8th note triplets. The palm-muted low notes act as a melodic and rhythm counterpoint.

The two left-hand taps on beat 4 of bar 4 give the right hand time to get into position for the tap at the very end of that bar.

Bars 9-10

This is the first of many sections that feature two-note motifs played to a triplet count. A similar approach is also taken in bars 11-12, 13-14, 33-36, 37-40, 43-46 and 47-48. Here, each two-note sixth motif is played a diatonic seventh interval apart from its predecessor.

I use inside picking starting on an upstroke and mainly alternate picking, however you can use hybrid picking if you prefer.

Bars 11-12

It will help you to play the rhythm of this section accurately if you think of the first notes in these two-note groups as tracing out an ascending 1/4 note triplet melody.

Again, although alternate picking is shown in the transcription, you can use hybrid picking if you prefer.

Bars 13-14

This section could be played using a succession of down-sweeps by refingering it, so that you place a different note on each string. However, you may find it more articulate and easier to play when fingered as shown. Each two-note sixth motif is again shifted up in intervals of a seventh.

Bars 15-16

I wanted to avoid too many clichéd country-style sixths using slides like this, but no sixth interval study would be complete without one.

Rhythmically, consecutive three-note groupings played to a triplet count will normally sound relatively straightforward, but this whole sequence has been displaced by an 1/8th note by starting on the second note of the first beat in bar 15.

Bars 19-20

This section contains a mixture of three- and two-note motifs mirroring the ascending country rock sequence in bars 15-16, but this time we descend.

It will help you play bar 20 more accurately if you think of the first notes of each group as tracing out a 1/4 note triplet melody as you did earlier.

Bars 21-22

It's possible to play each four-note motif in this passage using two taps in the left-hand followed by two taps in the right-hand, but you will again probably find it easier to finger it as written, as it involves fewer wide stretches.

Bar 24

Apart from the tone-wide trill between the D and E notes, this section is composed entirely of sixths.

Bars 25-26 (same as bars 29-30)

As a contrast to relentless single notes, this section uses some double-stops. These require moderately wide stretches, but it is also possible to adopt a more vertical approach by relocating the note on the B string in each pair to the G string.

The consecutive four-note groupings cause the motifs to be rhythmically displaced when played to a triplet count (producing a "4 against 3" effect).

Bars 27-28

These two bars require tapping two consecutive notes with each hand and, on each string-pair, features playing down one sixth interval and up then next.

Bars 31-32

During the "break" there is a succession of second inversion sixth arpeggios of G6, A6, D6, Em6 (all formed by stacking consecutive diatonic sixths). For each one, we play the sixth using a right-hand tap, then the root, third and fifth using the left hand.

Bars 33-36

Most of the remaining solo showcases a variety of approaches to using two-note sixth motifs that move in consecutive second intervals.

While the descending patterns in bars 11-12 doubled back on themselves as they ascended, the ones in bars 33-34 ascend in a single direction. As most of the notes are not played on adjacent strings, there is more work for your picking hand as you are having to skip strings throughout. Although I used alternate picking you might prefer hybrid picking using a middle-finger upstroke followed by a picked downstroke throughout.

In bar 35, we descend one sixth and ascend the next as we climb the neck with each motif played on an adjacent string pair.

In bar 36, we keep the same approach while descending the neck, and using string skips, rather than placing all the lower notes on the B string.

Bars 43-46

Next, a series of six-note groupings of sixths stacked in fourths snake up and down while ascending the neck. More rhythmic interest is created by starting the sequence on the final note of beat one which causes the groups to stagger over the bar lines and helps avoid predictability.

Although there is a mix of picks, hammer-ons, and slides, the spaces between each note should be even (so don't rush the slides).

Bars 47-48

There are more six-note groupings in this final section, this time starting on the downbeat, so there is no rhythmic displacement.

Like bars 11-12 and bar 20, the first notes in the consecutive series of two-note motifs trace out a 1/4 note triplet melody as they double back while inching down the neck.

I alternate picked this section, but you can use hybrid picking if you prefer.

DOZ
(Solo Study Featuring Sixth Intervals)

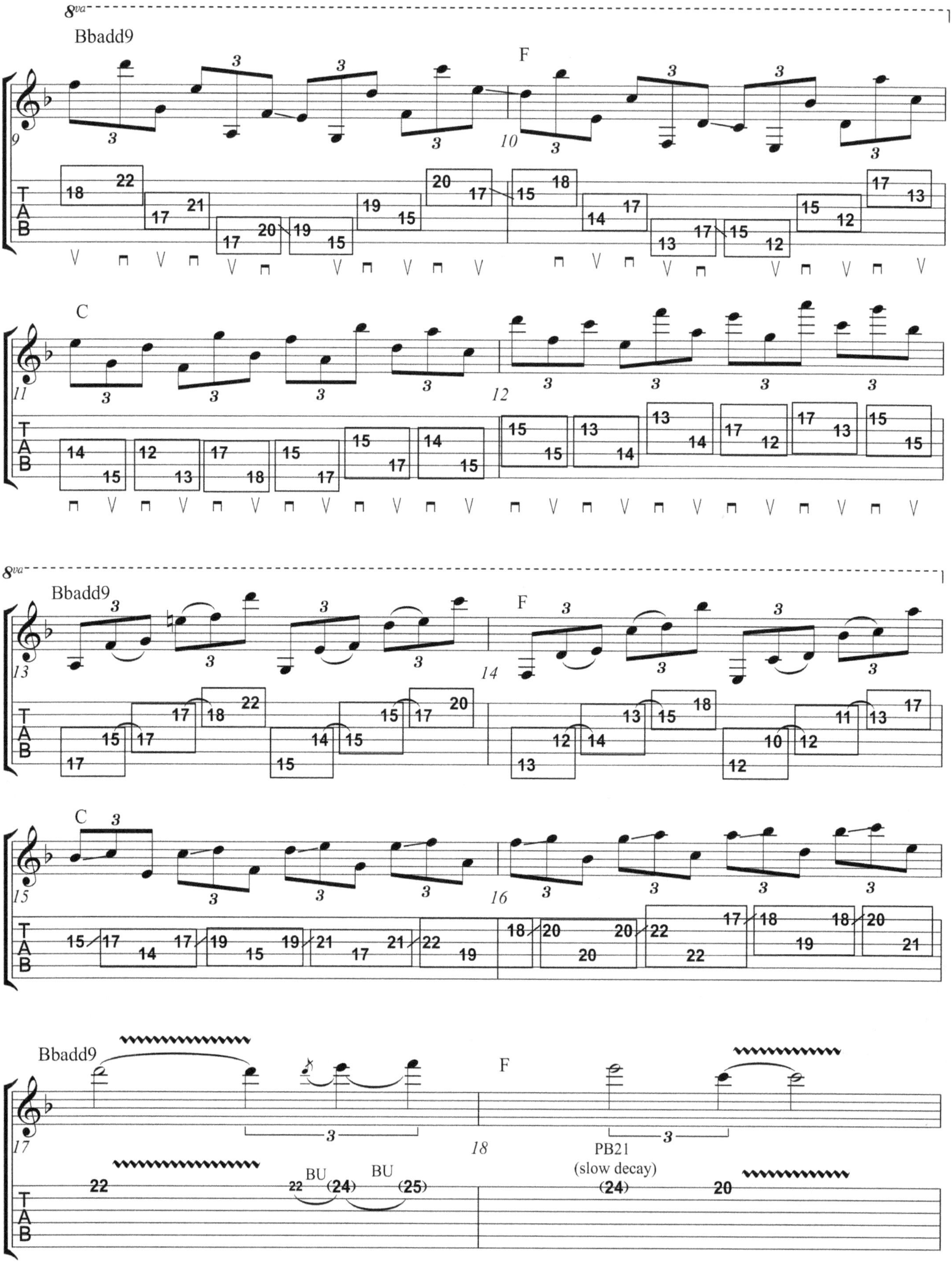
8va
Bbadd9
F
C
8va
Bbadd9
F
C
Bbadd9
F
BU
BU
PB21
(slow decay)

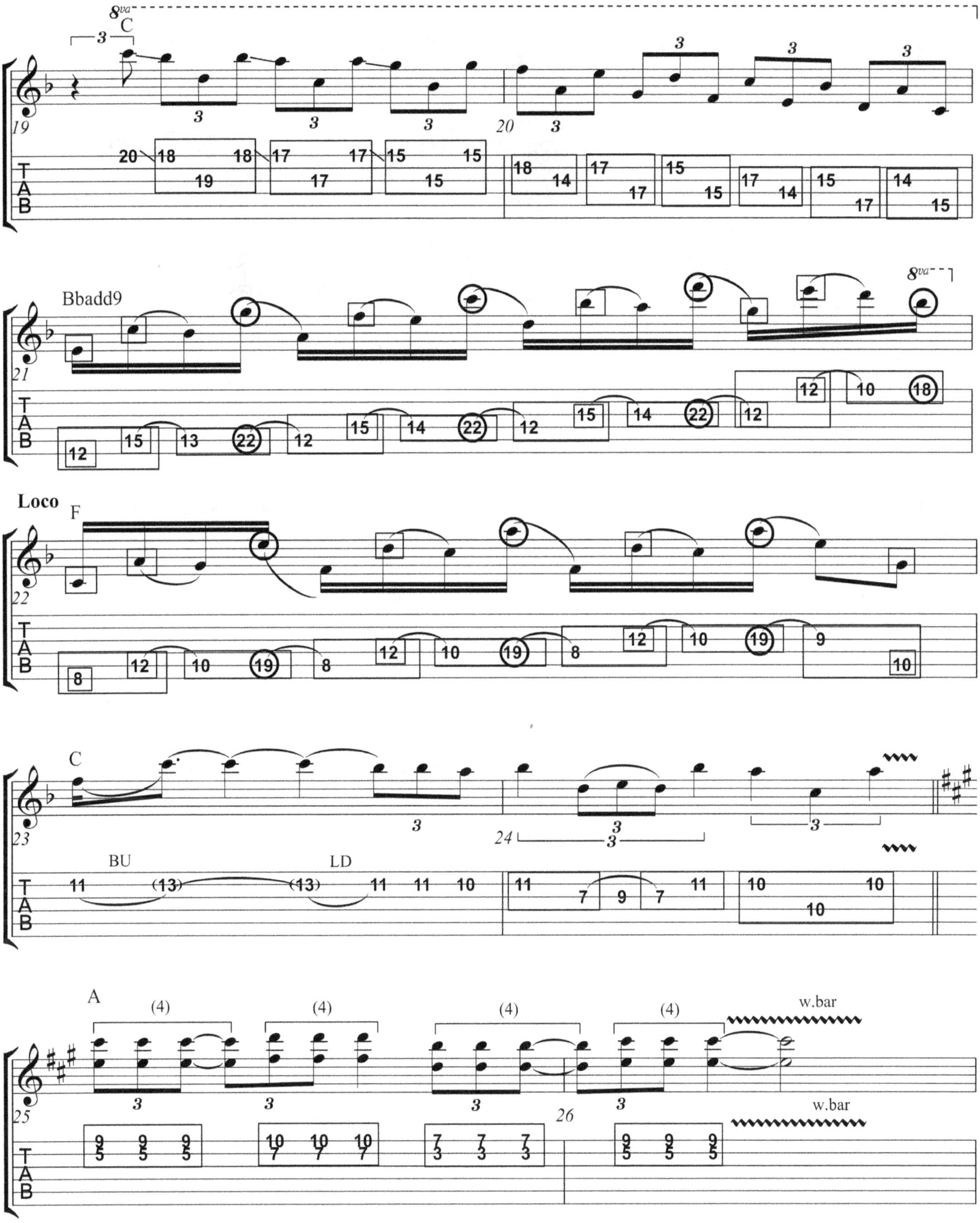
8va
C
Bbadd9
Loco
F
C
BU
LD
A
(4)
w.bar

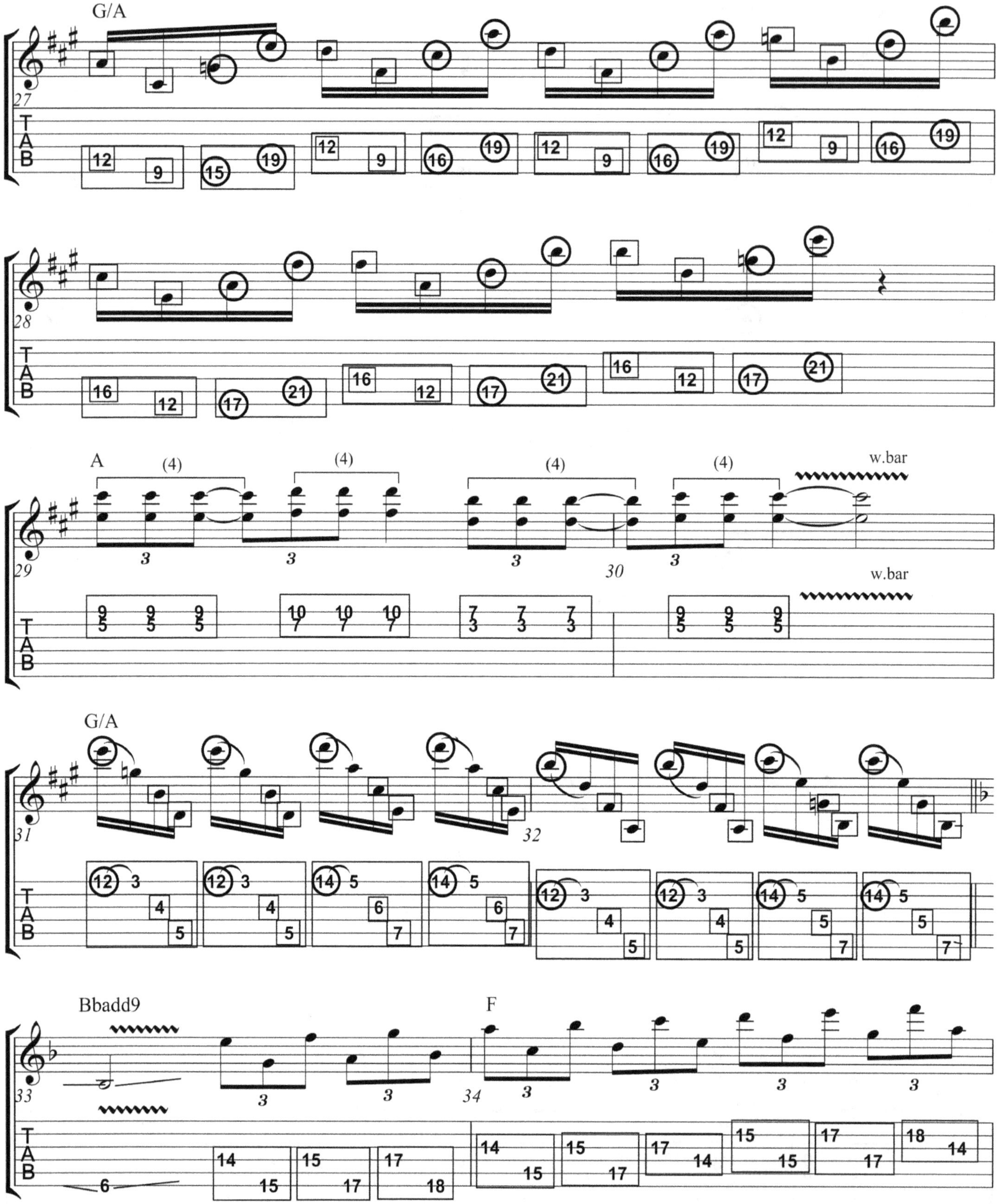
G/A
27
28
A
(4)
w.bar
29
30
G/A
31
32
Bbadd9
F
33
34

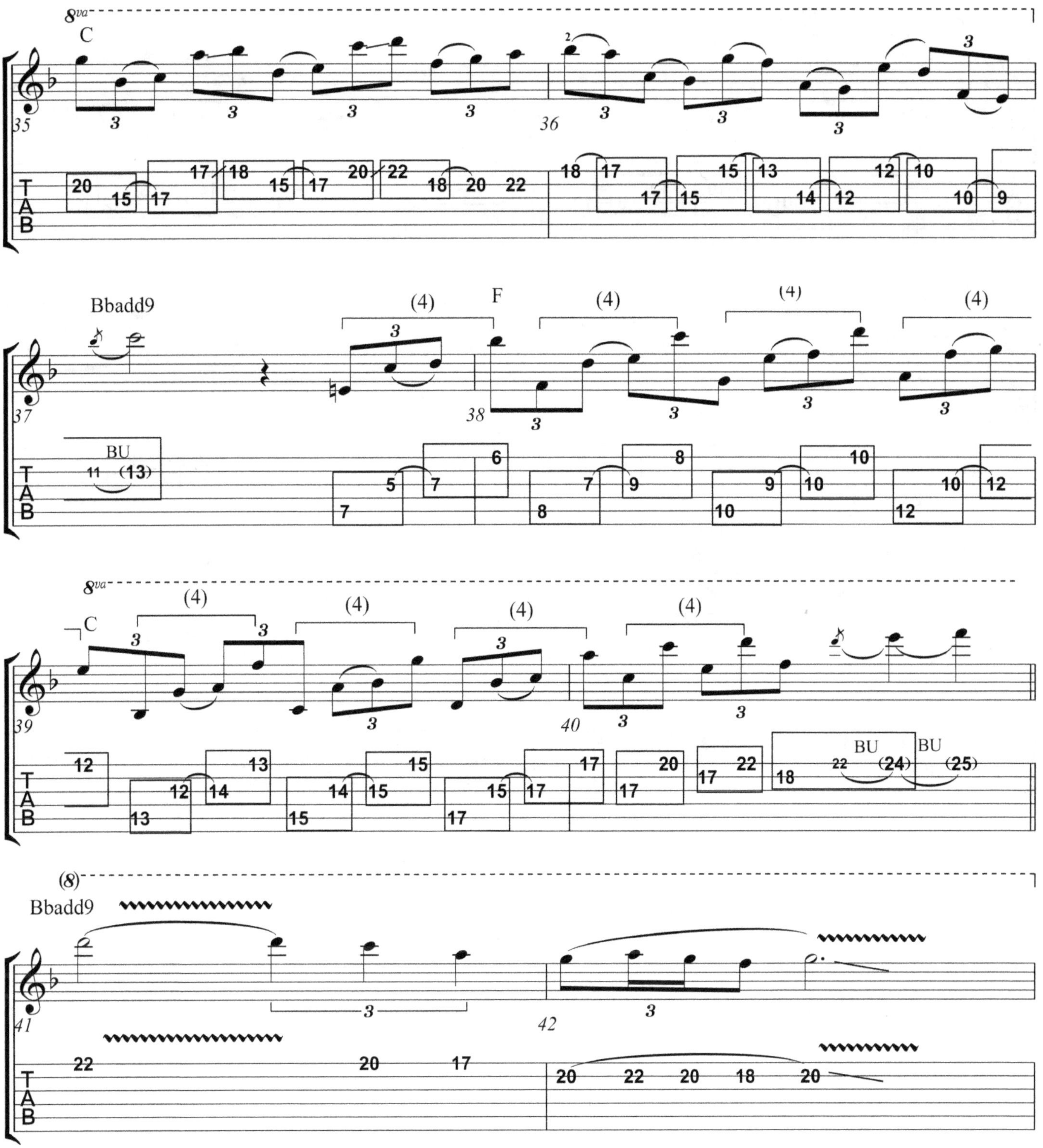
8va
C
Bbadd9
(4)
F
BU
8va
C
(4)
BU
(8)
Bbadd9

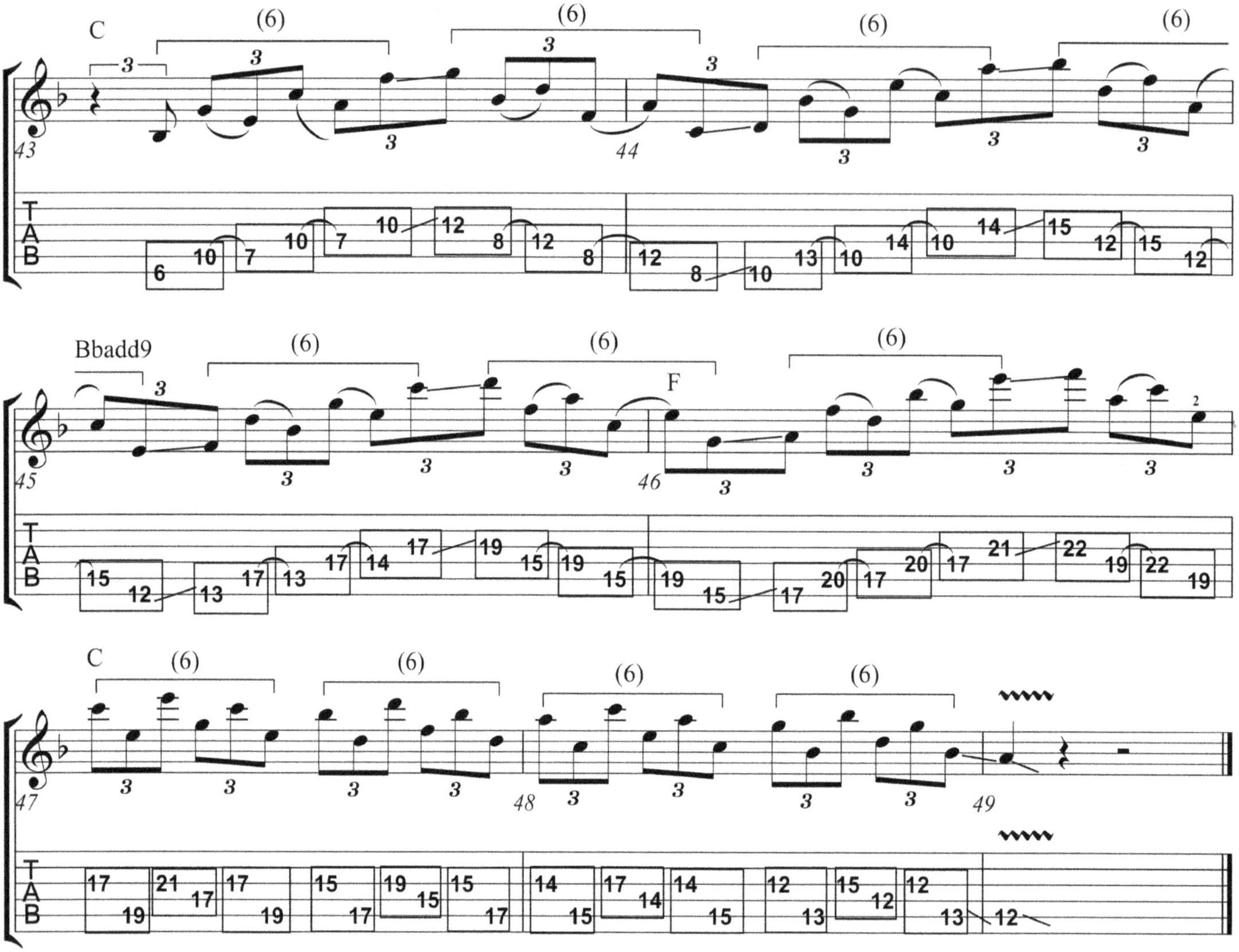
C
Bbadd9
F
C

Chapter Six: Seventh Intervals Solo Study

Musical Effect

Sevenths tend to sound quite dark and dissonant compared to other intervals.

Technical Considerations

The intervals have now become so wide that it is no longer feasible to play them on adjacent strings, so string skips and/or tapping are often the most practical options.

Solo Performance Notes

In the transcription certain notes have rectangular boxes around them.

- Rectangle around two notes = a single diatonic seventh interval

- Rectangle around three or more notes = multiple consecutive diatonic seventh intervals

Bar 1

Each four-note grouping in this bar is two seventh intervals played a sixth interval apart.

Bar 2

In this bar, rhythmic interest is created by alternating between two- and three-note groupings.

Bars 3-4

This section features five-note groupings, each based around a stack of seventh intervals (similar ideas can be seen in bars 17-18, 25-26, 37-40 and 41-44). When repeated to a triplet count, five-note groupings have a long and interesting rhythmic cycle with the point of emphasis changing throughout.

There are times (such as when using seventh intervals) when hybrid picking makes a lot of sense, as it significantly reduces the amount of work required from the picking hand. However, although hybrid picking is shown in the transcription for this and a few other sections, feel free to use a plectrum throughout if your picking is fast and accurate enough.

Note the use of lateral motion here. The ability to take any figure/motif "for a walk" like this is a great way of generating ideas and creating natural thematic development. The same approach is also used in bars 15-16, 17-18 and most of the second half of this solo.

Bar 5

This bar represents the opposite of bar 1. Again, we play four-note groupings comprising of two seventh intervals played a sixth interval apart, but where bar 1 featured two descending motifs followed by an ascending one, this bar contains two ascending ones followed by a descending one.

Bar 6

Rhythmically, things straighten out here as we play three-note groupings to a triplet count.

The left- and right-hand taps at the end of bar 6 help to take pressure off the right hand to get into position for the tapping sequence in the following two bars.

Bars 7-8

When certain shapes present convenient fingering opportunities, take them!

Convenient Seventh Interval Stack Fingering

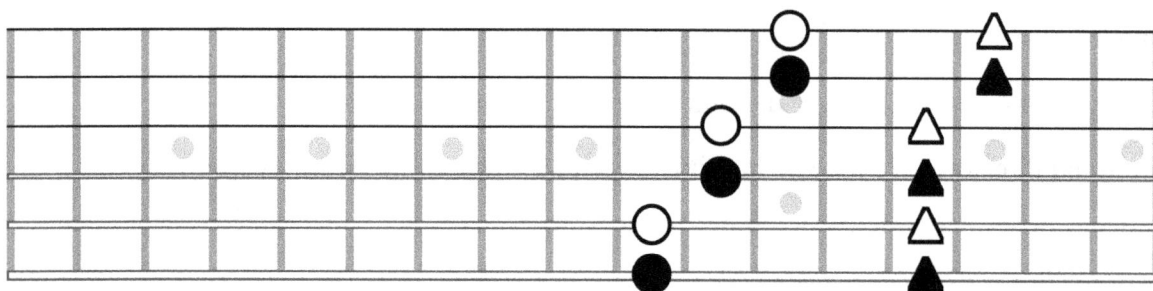

Look at the movement in these two bars (a four-note motif comprising two seventh intervals a third apart descending in fourths) and experiment with other variations, some of which can be seen in bars 12, 19-20, 29-30, 35-36 and 47-48.

This is the first of many passages where consecutive two-note groupings are played as triplets using left- and right-hand tapping. This will challenge your timing, so focus on playing everything as evenly and robotically as possible, and target the first note of each beat.

Bars 9-11

Most of this solo is a straightforward workout in 1/8th note triplets but these three bars show what can be achieved with some rhythmic variation. The mixture of left-hand tapping and hybrid picking makes it easier to transition from the right-hand tapped note at the start of bar 9.

Bar 12

There are more two-note permutations here: this time, alternating between "low to high" then "high to low".

Bars 13-14

Here, you'll play triple-picked consecutive ascending seventh intervals. Rhythmic interest is created by dividing the melody into groups of three beats which cut across the four beats in a bar arrangement. In other words, 3/4 against 4/4.

Bars 15-16

In this passage, we see a flipped version of the figure used in bar 6. This time the configuration is "high-low-high". Have fun with the sevenths played as angry double-tops at the end of bar 16!

Bars 17-18

In bar 17, a three-note stack of ascending sevenths is followed by another a fourth higher. The process is then reversed in the second half of the bar before the same configuration is repeated in the following bar.

Don't rush the straight 1/8th note triplets when playing the slides.

Bars 19-20

Here, two-note permutations are arranged to create six-note groupings by reversing the third pair each time (creating a low to high, low to high, high to low configuration). This approach also works well if flipped to descend the scale (using high to low, high to low, low to high).

Bars 21-24

This section mainly acts as a melodic respite from the relentless barrage of consecutive sevenths.

Bars 25-26

These two bars are a flipped version of the shapes used in bars 17-18, with each half-bar theme doubling-back throughout as we steadily move up the fingerboard.

Note how the rhythm and melody of the right-hand taps is accentuated in the backing track. This helps to give meaningful detail to what could otherwise be a featureless stream of unrelenting 1/8th note triplets.

Bars 27-28

There are more five-note groupings here. Focus on the notes on the B string as they beat out an interesting rhythm that gives this section its internal groove.

Bars 29-30

Here, each seventh interval motif is paired with another a fourth lower.

Bars 33-34

Apart from the slide from G to A at the start of bar 34, the melody in this section is composed entirely of diatonic sevenths.

Bars 37-39

This section uses the same three-note stacked forms as bars 17-18 and 25-26. Each is separated by a single note producing a succession of four-note groupings which rhythmically displace as they are played as triplets.

Bars 41-44

More three-note stacked forms – this time repeated and descending through the scale to trace out a "castle wall" pattern with a combination of left- and right-hand tapping.

Bar 46

This bar contains a descending version of the movement used in bars 16-17.

Bars 47-48

To help with the rhythm of this final passage, focus on the 1/4 note triplet traced out by the first note in each of the two-note groups.

SEVENTH HEAVEN
(Solo Study Featuring Seventh Intervals)

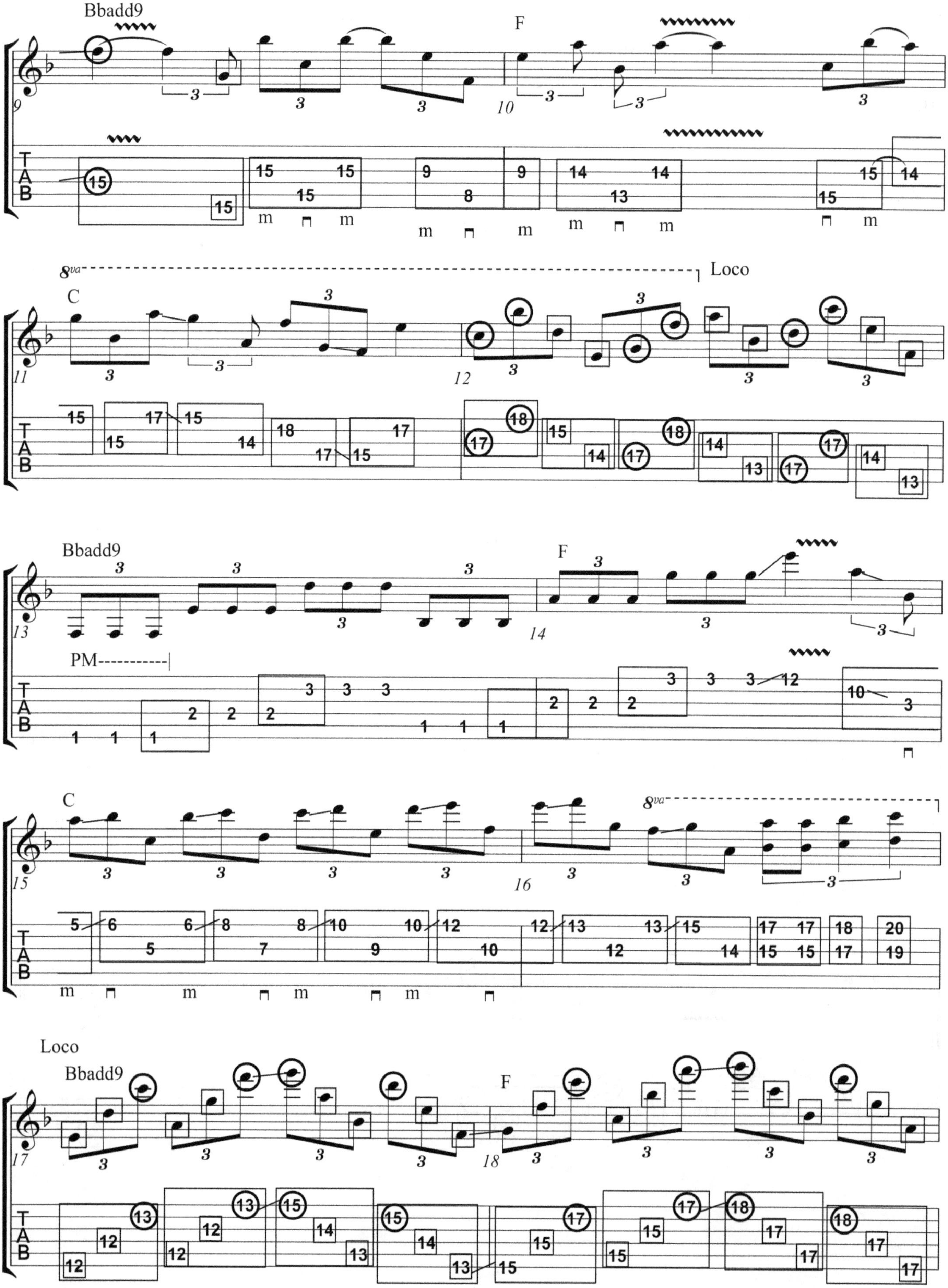
Bbadd9
F
8va
Loco
C
Bbadd9
F
PM
C
8va
Loco
Bbadd9
F

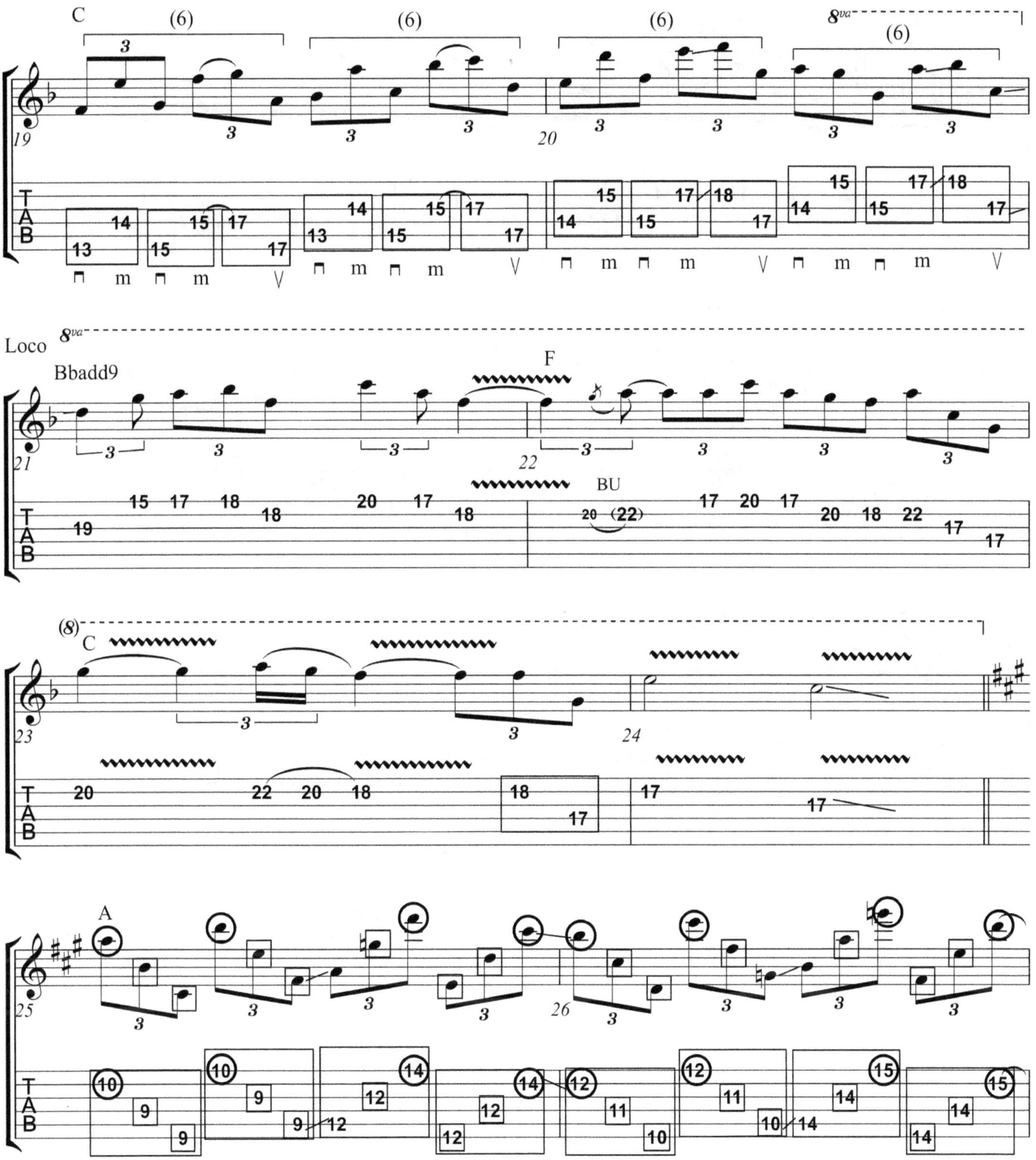
C
(6)
8va
Loco
Bbadd9
F
BU
(8)
A

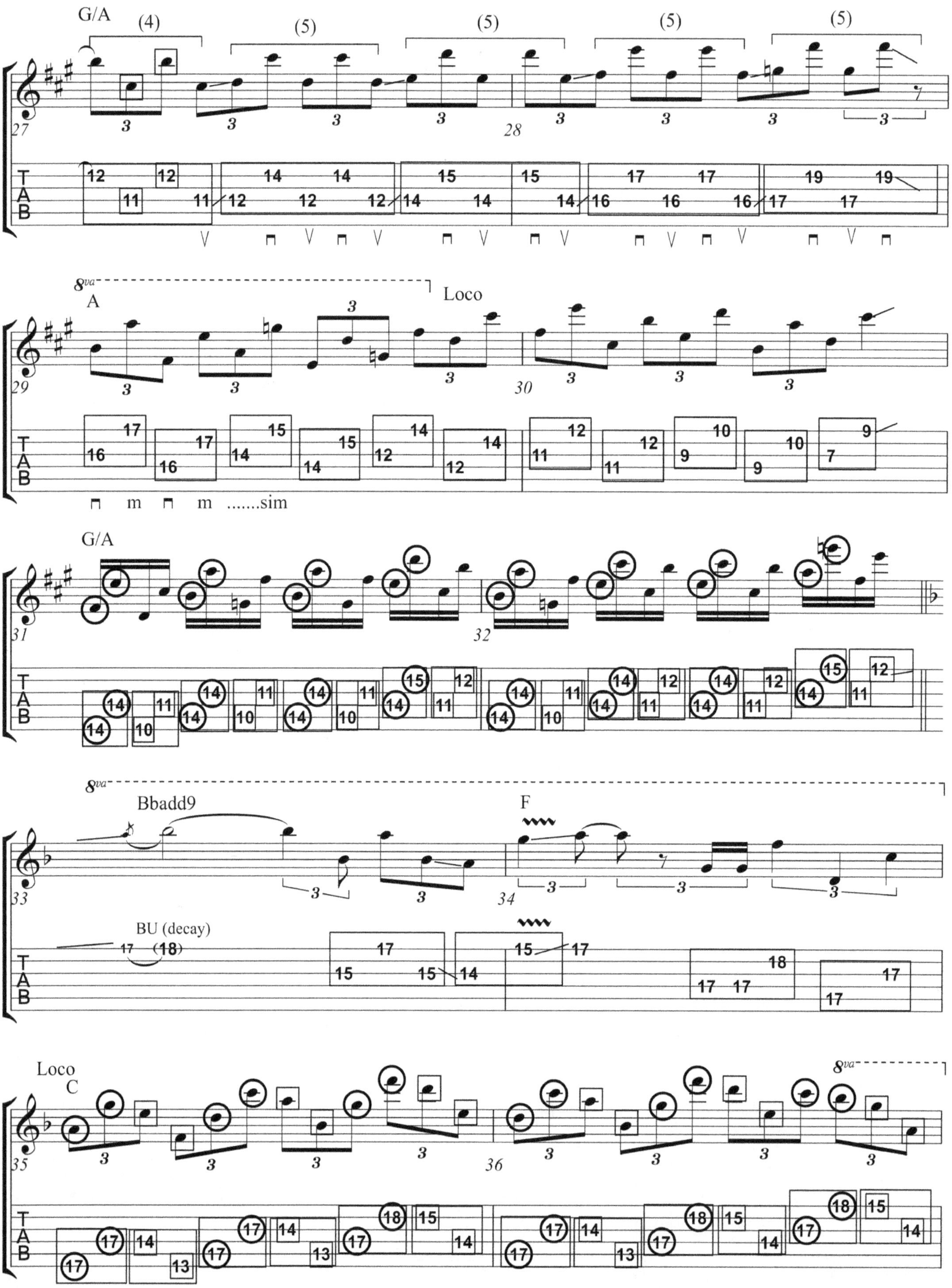
G/A
(4)
(5)
(5)
(5)
(5)
8va
A
Loco
m m ....sim
G/A
8va
Bbadd9
F
BU (decay)
Loco
C
8va

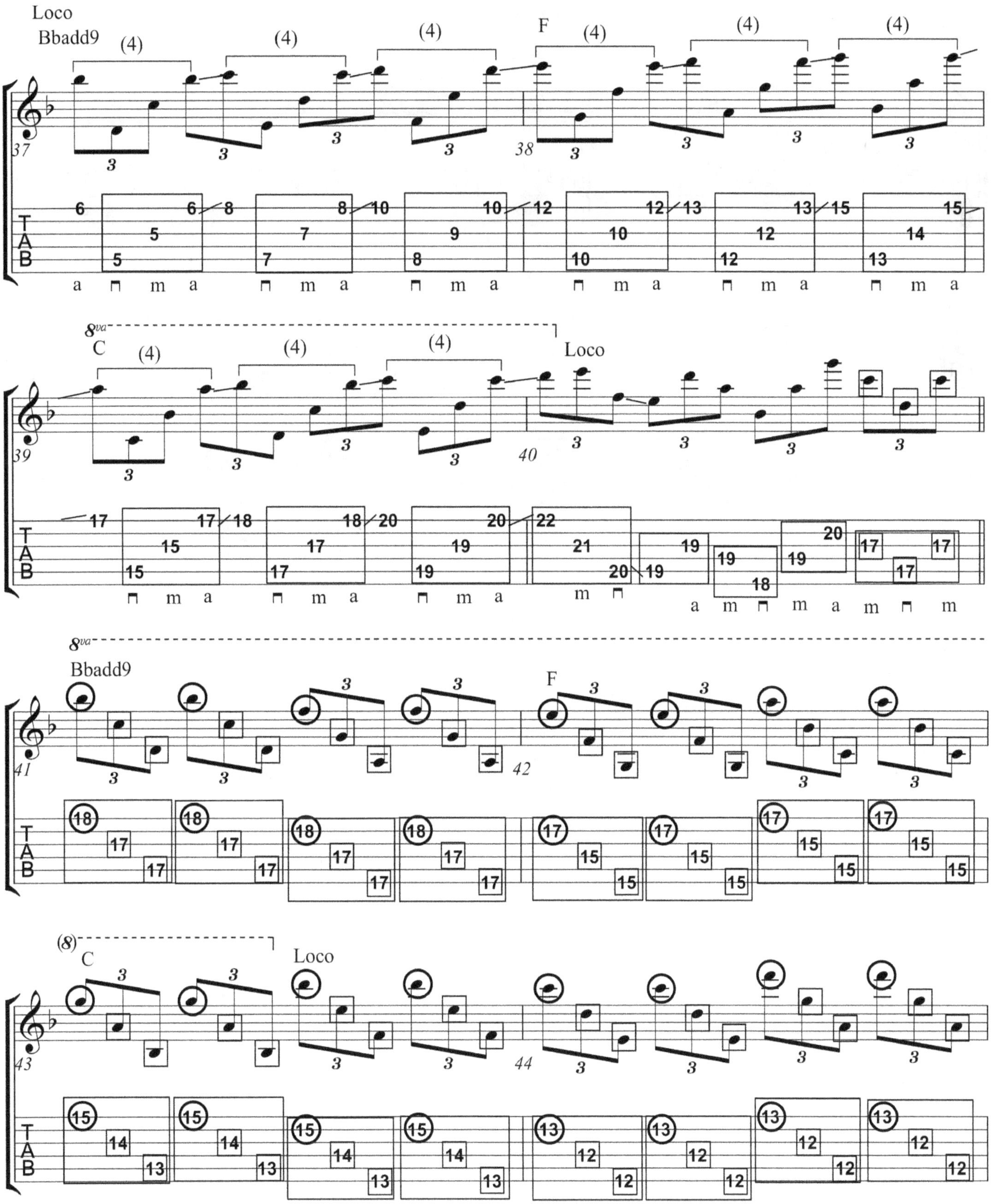
Loco
Bbadd9
F
8va
C
Loco
8va
Bbadd9
F
(8)
C
Loco

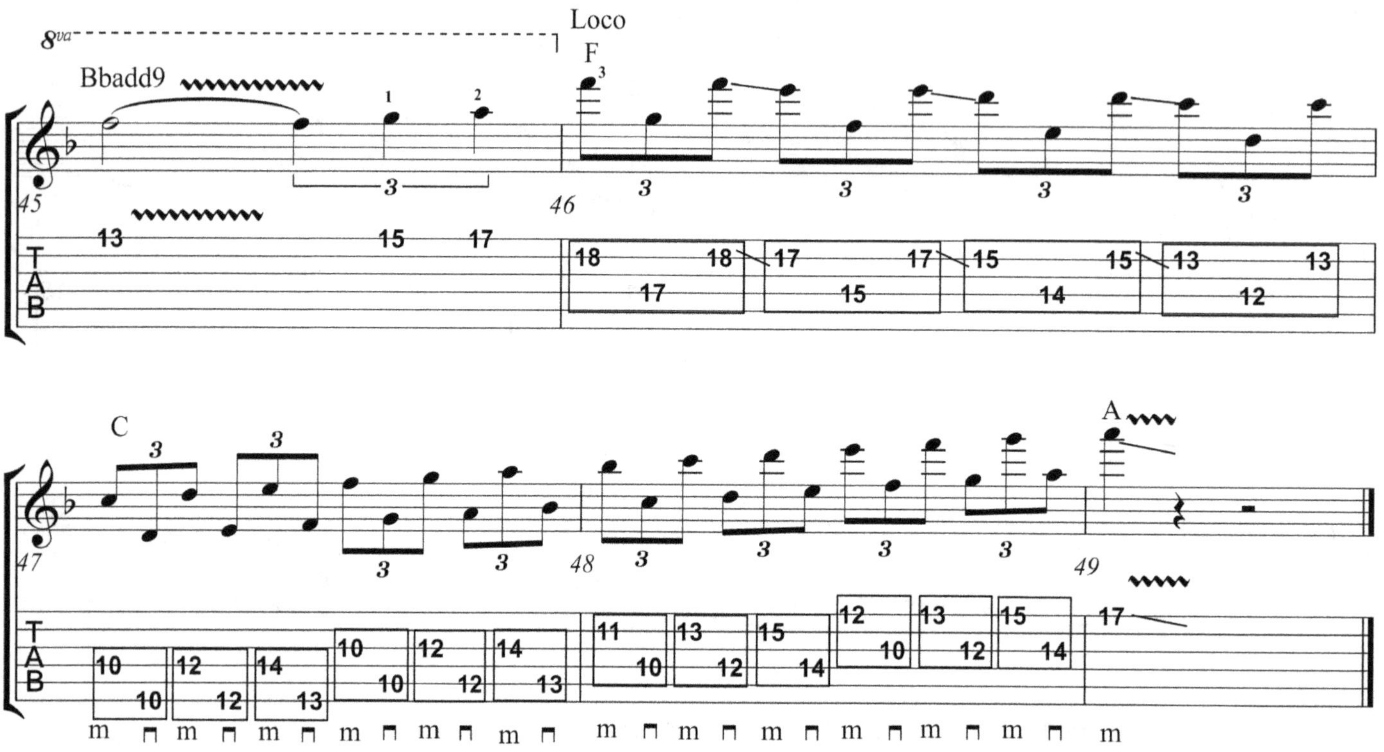
8va
Loco
Bbadd9
F
C
A
TAB

Chapter Seven: Octave Intervals Solo Study

Musical Effect:

Octaves tend to sound pure, clean, and strident. The sonic waveforms created by playing octaves are more stable and less dissonant than other intervals, and work well when played as double-stops using distortion.

Technical Considerations

Octave shapes are consistent for all notes (although you will still need to adapt for the tuning difference between the G and B strings) which makes it easy to right-hand tap a pattern that mirrors the fretting hand an octave higher.

Solo Performance Notes

The rectangular boxes around the notes in the transcription mean the following:

- Rectangle around two notes = a single octave interval

- Rectangle around three or more notes = multiple consecutive octave intervals

Bars 1-3

The motifs in bars 1-2 feature the same note stacked over two octaves. The first two notes of each of the six-note groups (E, A, D, G) are a fourth apart and a similar approach is also used in bars 25-26 and 30.

Using the economy-picked option as written involves playing a series of "skip sweeps", where consecutive downstrokes are played using one constant motion that involves jumping over a string. When doing this, the trajectory is similar to a stone skimming on the water: travelling constantly forward as it bounces.

Skip-Sweep Action (constant forward motion)

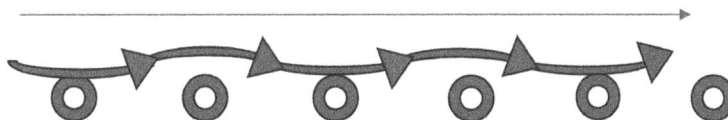

Bar 3 contains octaves shifted up in scale steps.

Bar 4

Intervallic motifs can be shifted in combinations of intervals. For example, here the initial octave motif shifts up a fourth, then down a second, down a fourth, down a second, and up a fourth as it traces a "castle wall" style motion.

Analyse the motion of other examples in this solo study before experimenting with variations of your own (for example, bar 7 sees each octave motif shifted up a fourth and this same principle is then shifted up in seconds, ascending laterally up the neck).

Bars 5-6

In this passage, octave motifs are shifted down in seconds over a pedal note played using a right-hand tap.

Bar 8

As in bar 1, here are more two-octave forms, this time played on adjacent strings using a combination of open strings and right-hand taps to produce a wide interval spread in a confined physical area.

Bars 11-12

Here, the initial motif is followed by another a sixth higher. This pairing is then shifted up a fourth before sliding up a tone for the reverse (a descending octave motif followed by another a sixth lower).

You'll learn a lot from analysing the motion in bars 25-26, 27-28, 30, 37 and 43-44.

Bars 13-14

The shifting octaves in this passage include left-hand taps and whammy bar scoops for more expression.

Bar 15

Now the octaves are played as double-stops, a common approach in both rock and jazz. The same idea is used in bars 22-24 and 38.

Bar 29

The first six-note motif in this bar shows the same note played in four different pitches and spread over three octaves. It is then shifted up a fourth.

Bar 31

Here, the right-hand taps trace out a 1/4 note triplet rhythm.

Using right-hand taps up an octave from some of the notes played with the left hand is a great way of adding some glitter to a line. A similar approach is used in bars 31 and 35-36 (a passage that also uses slides for an even more ear-catching effect).

Bar 32

In this section, the right-hand taps trace out an 1/8th note rhythm.

Bars 33-43

These bars feature "call and response" where the same idea is played in two different octaves on the same string. It's an approach often used by Yngwie Malmsteen and echoes the stylings of violin virtuoso Niccolò Paganini.

Bars 37-38

Here, we see an approach often used by Tosin Abasi (which he refers to as "selective picking") where the same note is played with both left-hand tapping and picking for a combination of tonal interest and physical ease when crossing strings.

Bars 39-40

Interest is created here by shadowing what is played in the left-hand by tapping notes an octave higher.

Bars 41-42

A brief but hard tap on the fret wire 12 frets higher than a fretted note produces a pure ringing harmonic and is shown in bar 42. This approach was often used by Eddie Van Halen.

Bars 43-44

A combination of techniques is used to play this passage cleanly at speed with good tone. While you could pick every note here, would it sound as nice?

Bars 47-48

We conclude with a line that contains a moving single note over a stationary (pedal) octave.

8 BALL
(Solo Study Featuring Octave Intervals)

(Half-time triplet feel)

(Shaun Baxter)

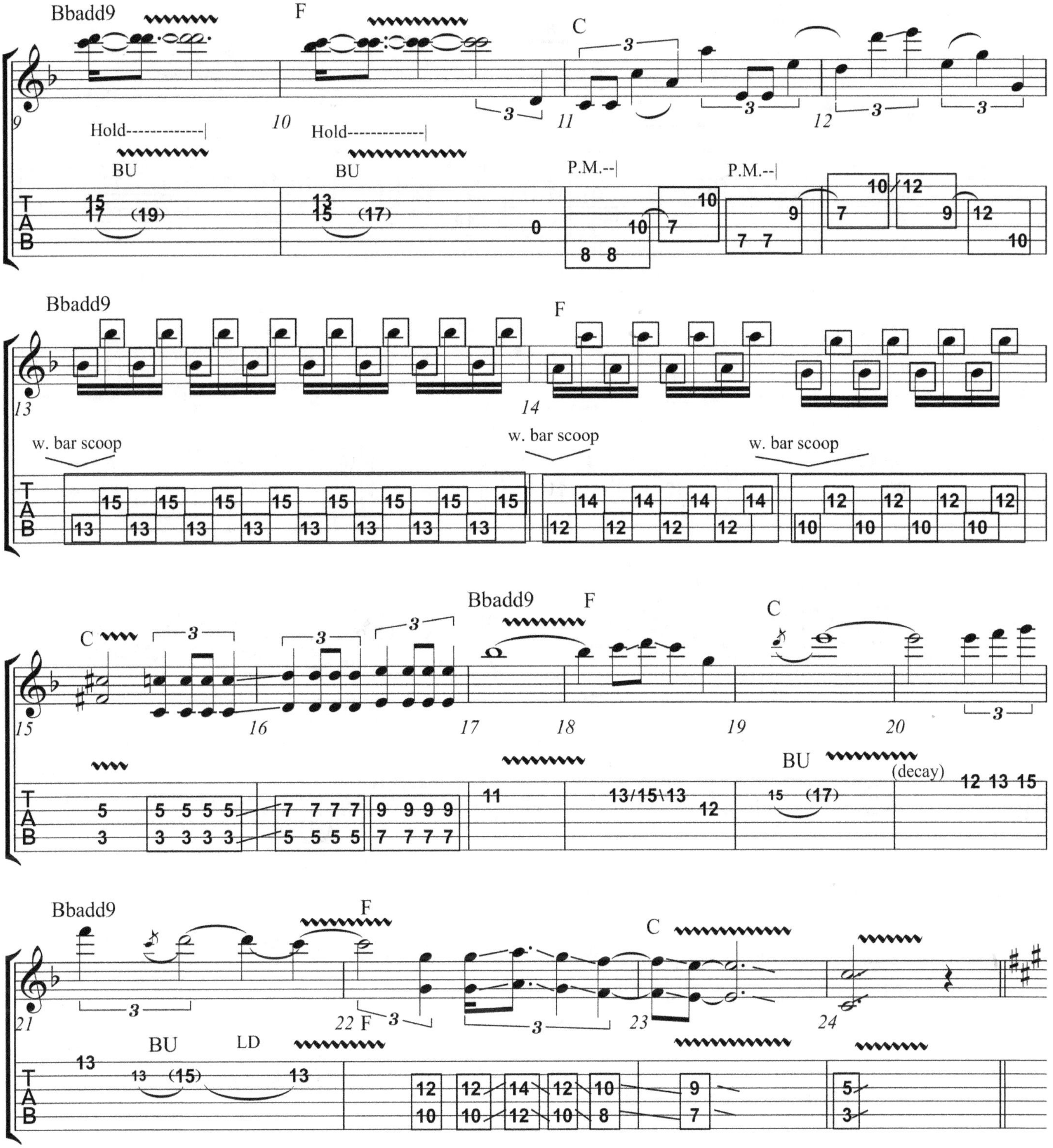
Bbadd9
F
C
Hold
BU
P.M.
Bbadd9
F
w. bar scoop
w. bar scoop
w. bar scoop
Bbadd9
F
C
C
BU
(decay)
Bbadd9
F
C
BU
LD
F

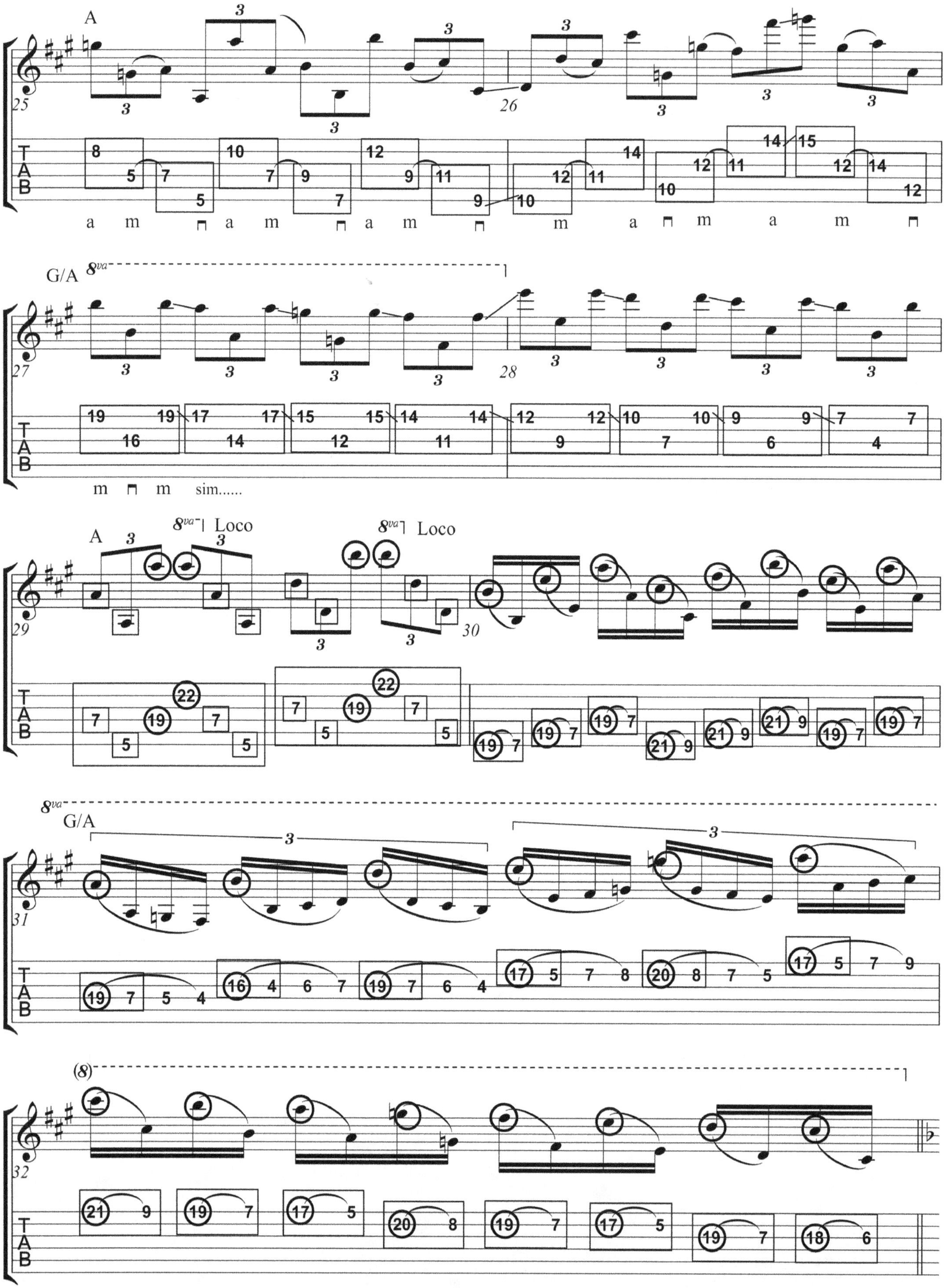
A
G/A
8va
m ⊓ m sim......
A
8va Loco
8va Loco
G/A
(8)

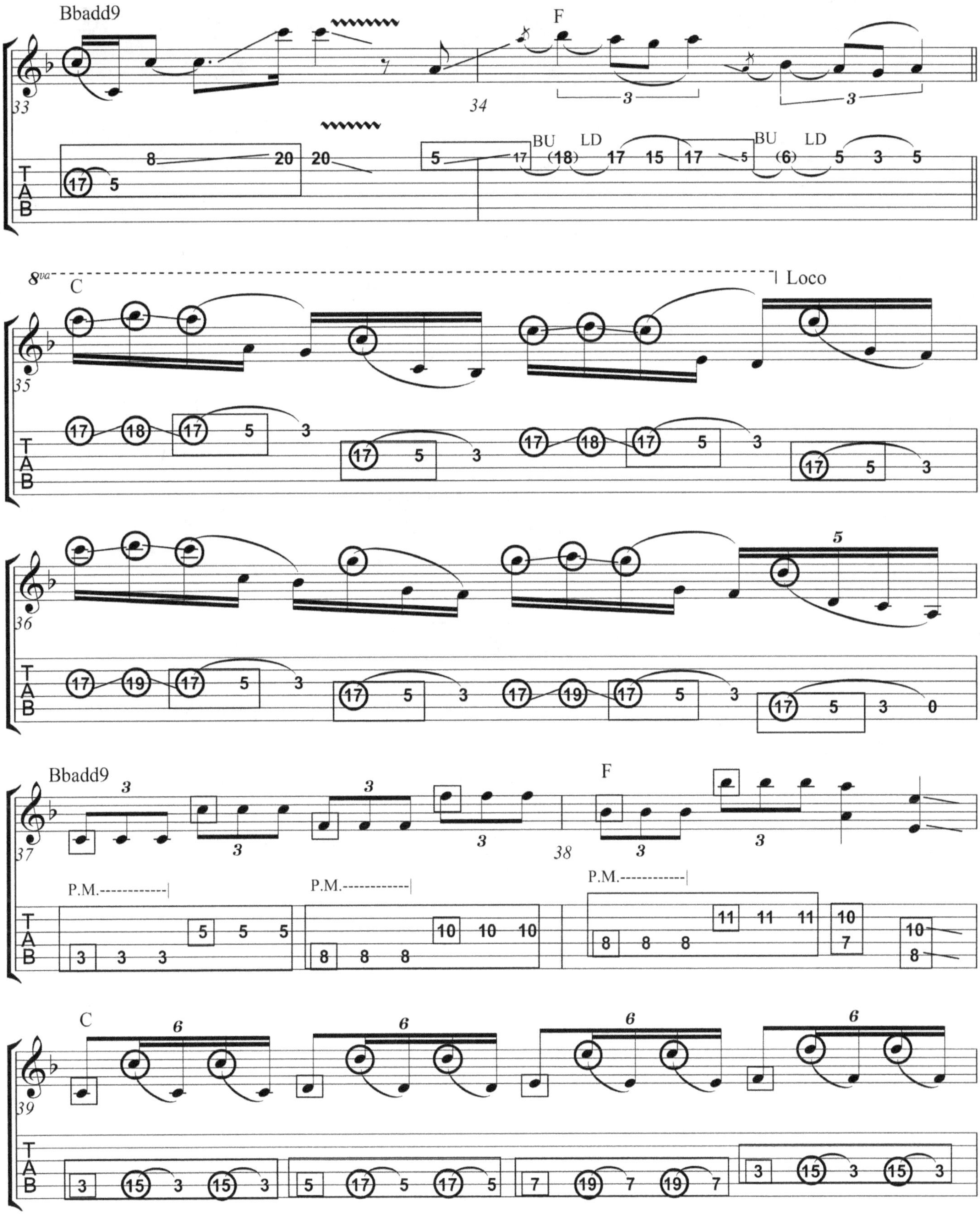
Bbadd9
F
BU
LD
8va
C
Loco
Bbadd9
P.M.
F
C

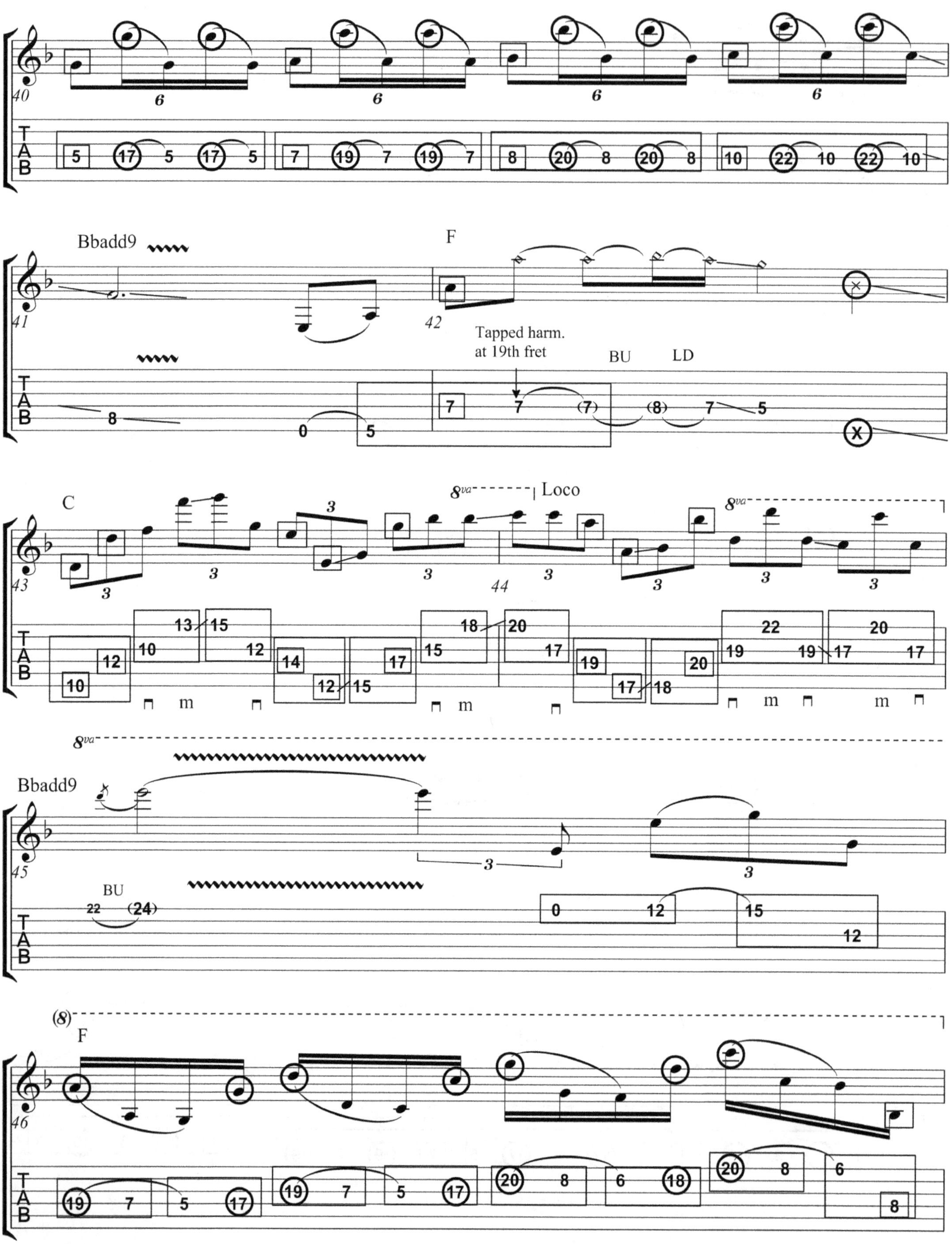
Bbadd9
F
Tapped harm.
at 19th fret
BU
LD
C
Loco
Bbadd9
BU
F

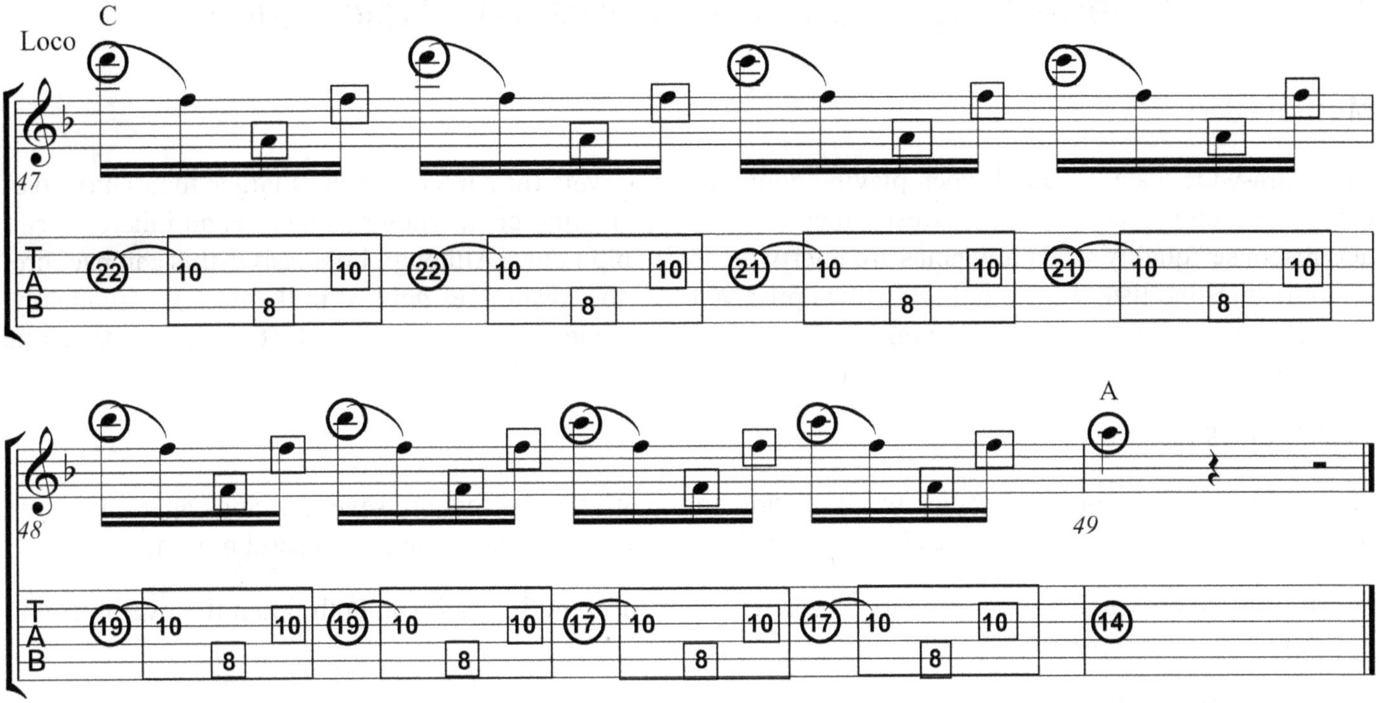
Loco
C
47
48
A
49

Chapter Eight: Compound Intervals Solo Study

Musical Effect

The extra-wide leaps required when playing compound intervals (any interval that is larger than an octave) can create quite whacky lines. However, they're great for creating counterpoint as there is an inherent "call and response" quality when low notes are intertwined with high ones. Although impressive, this can backfire, as sometimes the listener will only hear the upper voice as the lower ones get lost in the mix. Consequently, intricate parts using compound intervals may work best in a sparse musical setting to let the lower notes shine through too.

Technical Issues

Hybrid Picking is an obvious choice when playing consecutive notes that are several strings apart, although high up on the neck some wide stretches combined with string skips can be another useful option.

When using hybrid picking, it's good to experiment with palm muting as it can both fatten the overall sound and help with note separation.

Solo Performance Notes

In the transcription you'll notice that some notes have rectangular boxes around them.

- Rectangle around two notes = a single diatonic compound interval

- Rectangle around three or more notes = multiple consecutive diatonic compound intervals

Bars 1-2

This study begins with consecutive pairs of tenths played with some large stretches. Although technically challenging, I found this produced better results than if I placed the notes on strings that were further apart and relied on hybrid picking. There was something about the legato element that made the whole thing sound smoother.

Although the intervals are shown in pairs, each musical motif is built from four notes (with three motifs per bar) which creates an interesting cross rhythm when played as 1/8th note triplets.

Bars 3-4

Next, we play consecutive pairs of fourteenth intervals. Notice how the high notes are the main focus and produce a spikey melody and rhythm. The bass guitar and bass drum pattern have been synced to the lower notes to create an infectious rhythmic counterpoint.

Bars 5-6

These two bars are built from a series of three-note motifs each composed of a fifteenth followed by an octave.

The nested tuplet rhythm involves beating out a 1/4 note triplet rhythm with the right-hand tapped notes. If you focus on doing this, everything else should fall rhythmically into place.

Bars 7-8

In this section a series of twelfths motifs are slid up the neck.

Bars 9-18

This section uses a combination of tenths, elevenths, twelfths and thirteenths played as double-stops.

The second note in bar 18 shows an approximation of a technique used by saxophonists called "multiphonics". On the saxophone, this involves playing a high note while simultaneously generating a lower harmonic. On guitar, this can be mimicked by playing a high note (often with a bend or whammy bar scoop) while hammering onto a note on a lower string.

Bars 19-20

In bar 19, the first four notes are two tenth intervals a fifth apart. In the second half of the bar, this structure is shifted up a fourth. In bar 20, the same principle is used down a tone in C Mixolydian.

Bars 21-22

The first half of bar 21 features a variation on the four-note idea in bars 1-2. This time, we're using ninths instead of tenths, and each motif is six notes instead of four.

Pay attention to this six-note motif. It moves down a tone in the second half of bar 21 before the whole bar is repeated down a fourth in C Mixolydian.

Bars 23-24

To thicken the sound of the bend, a note an eleventh below is played also using a left-hand tap.

Bars 25-26

This two-bar section is effectively a reverse of the four-note motifs used in bars 1-2, again using ninths instead of tenths.

Bars 27-28

Make a note of how motifs in this solo are shifted in the scale while being adjusted to stay in key. Here, we trace out an ascending "castle wall" style movement as the original three-note motif is shifted up the neck.

Bars 29-30

Apart from adding expression and nuance, the slides linking these tenths help to take pressure off our picking hand.

Bars 31-32

These bars feature a rhythmically displaced version of the structures used in bars 27-28, this time using tenths instead of elevenths.

Bars 33-40

These atmospheric arpeggiations are based on tenths played an octave apart with left- and right-hand taps.

The final C# in bar 40 is a chromatic lead-in note to D, the third of the following Bb chord.

Bars 41-44

It's difficult to hear the extent of the rhythmic counterpoint in the baroque-tinged section (built from tenths and fifths) as most of the listener's attention is captured by the high notes. If this part was unaccompanied, the detail would be much more apparent.

Bars 46-47

This simple melody uses scale steps and is a contrast to the unrelenting compound intervals used so far.

Bars 47-49

In each of these two bars, the first four-note motif is built from two tenth intervals a seventh apart. It is then played a fourth higher, before sliding up a second into a descending equivalent.

LEVIATHAN
(Solo Study Featuring Compound Intervals)

G/A
12ths
P.M.
P.M.
P.M.
P.M.
P.M.
P.M.
Bbadd9
F
C
12ths
w.bar scoop
13th
12ths
13th
Bbadd9
F
C
12ths
w.bar scoop
13ths
w.bar doop
10ths
w.bar scoop

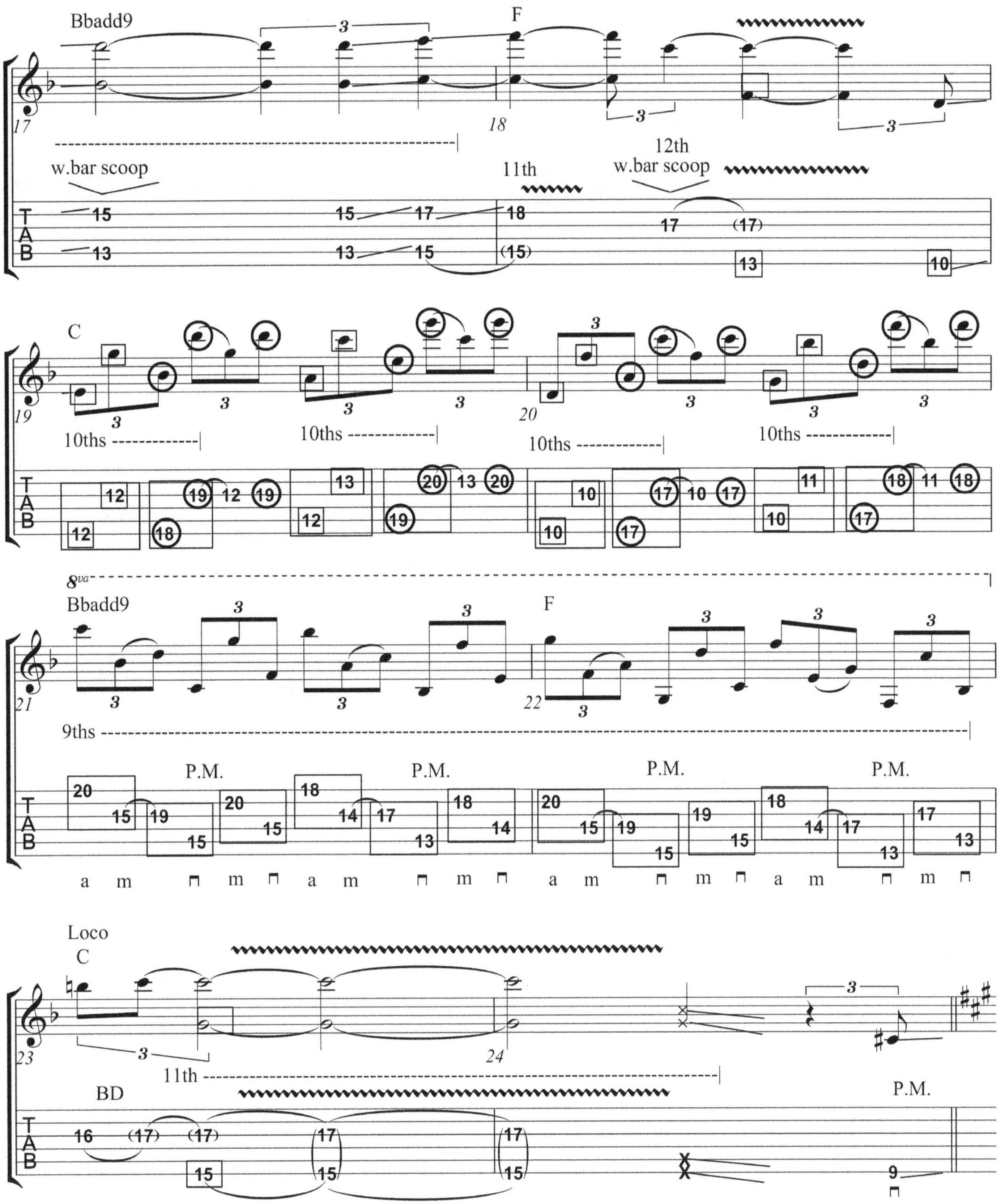
Bbadd9
F
w.bar scoop
11th
12th
w.bar scoop
C
10ths
8va
9ths
P.M.
a m m a m m a m m a m m
Loco
11th
BD

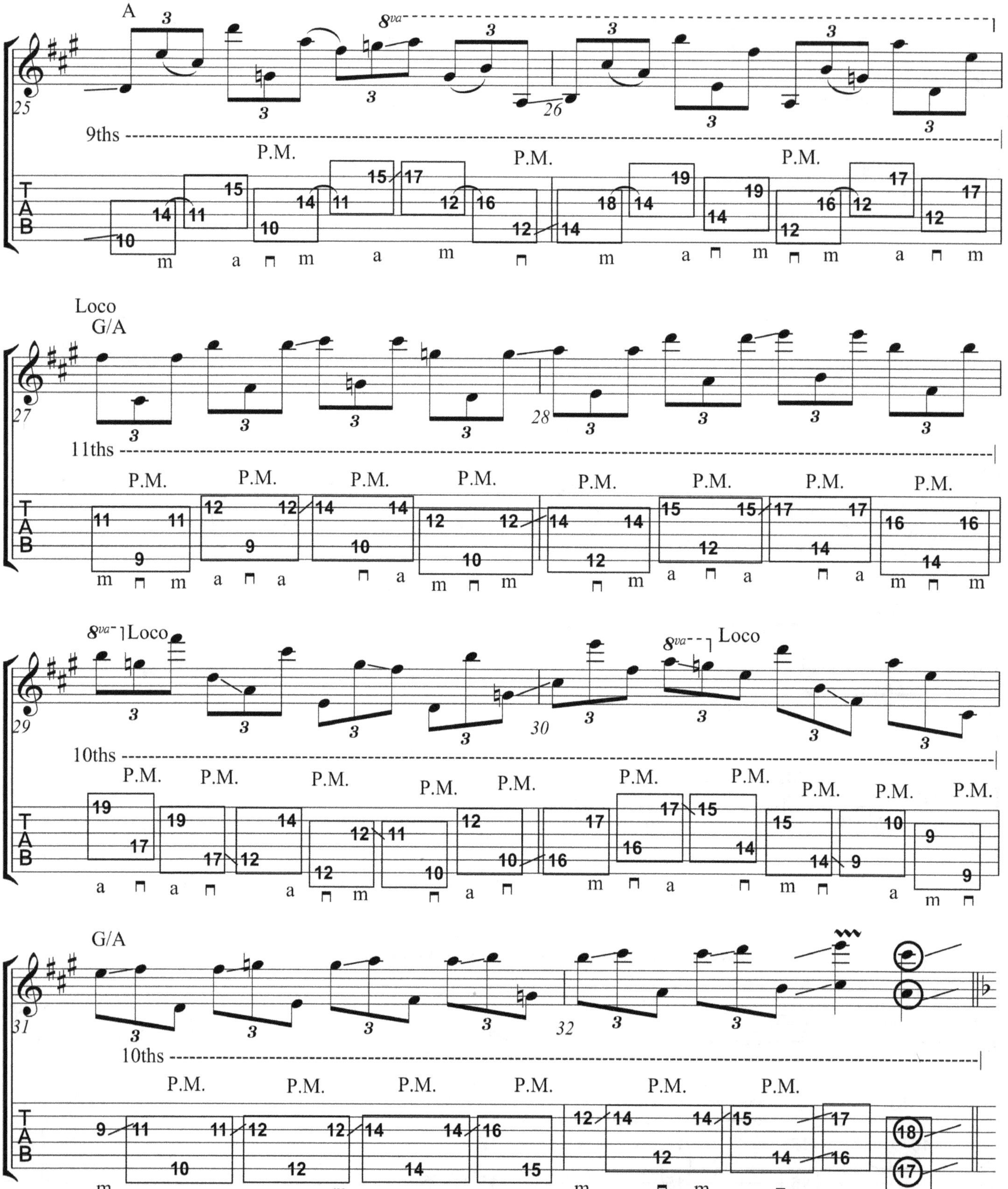
A
8va
9ths
P.M.
Loco
G/A
11ths
10ths

Bbadd9
F
C
10ths
Bbadd9
F
C
8va
Bbmaj7(no 5th)
Em7b5(no 5th)
Am7(no 5th)
Dm7(no 5th)
Gm7(no 5th)
C7(no 5th)
10ths & 5ths
P.M.
m a sim............
Loco
Fmaj7(no 5th)
Bbmaj7(no 5th)
Bbadd9
F

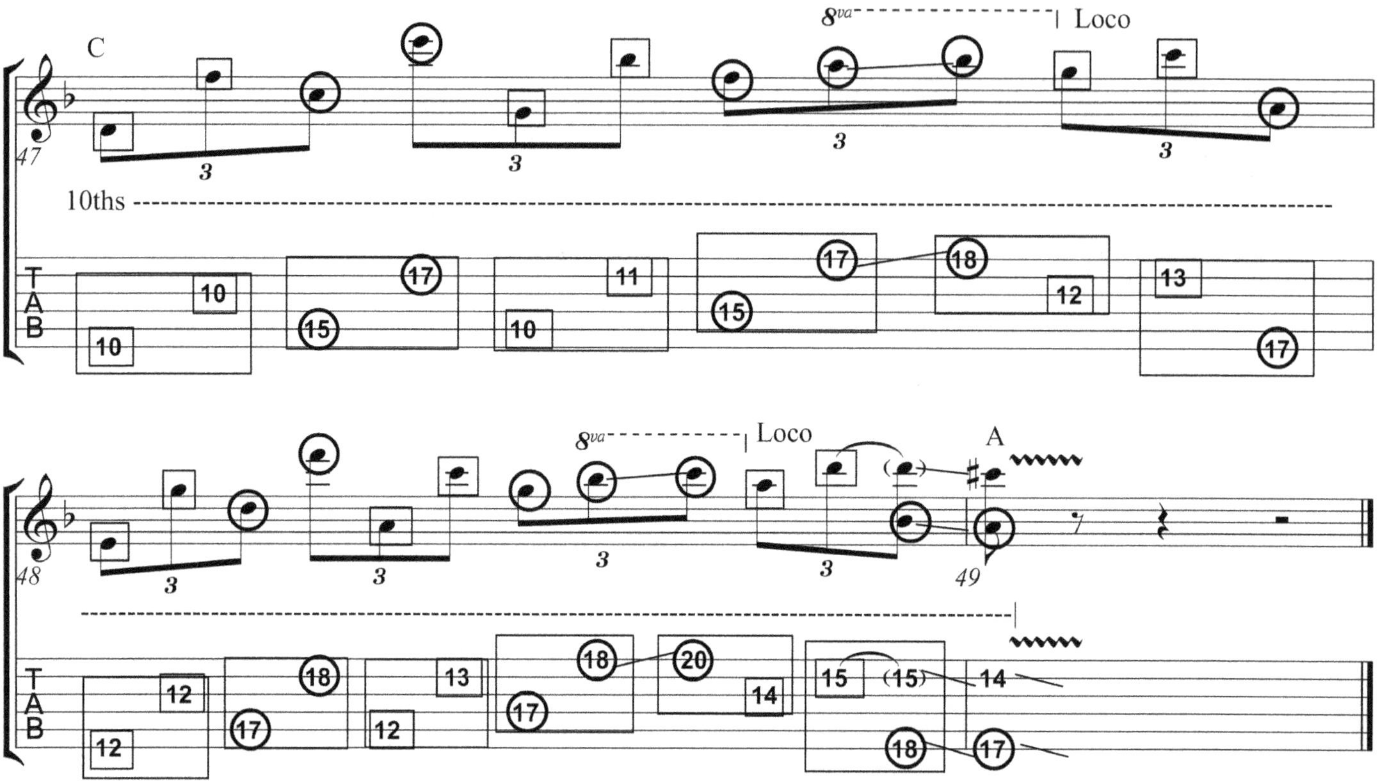
C
8va
Loco
10ths
8va
Loco
A

Chapter Nine: Mixed Intervals Solo Study One

Musical Effect

Until now, we've focused exclusively on one interval type in each solo, but in the final two chapters we will combine all the simple and compound interval types into two comprehensive solos. As you might expect, the musical results will be more blended.

With experience, you will start to hear and feel the musical effects of each interval, and this will help you to have more control over both the melody and mood of your playing. In broad terms, you could categorise and group the various interval types as follows:

- **Seconds, thirds, sixths, tenths** and **thirteenths** = soft and melodic

- **Fourths, fifths, elevenths** and **twelfths** = hard and angular

- **Sevenths, ninths** and **fourteenths** = dissonant and quirky

- **Octaves** and **fifteenths** = consonant and sweet

Technical Considerations

The final two solo studies require us to use the full array of technical approaches at our disposal!

Solo Performance Notes

As usual, in the transcription some notes have rectangular boxes around them.

- Rectangle around two notes = a single diatonic interval

- Rectangle around three or more notes = multiple consecutive diatonic intervals

This solo provides an opportunity to hear how various intervallic approaches and interval types contrast in the same musical setting. It includes bigger structures created from combinations of different intervals, and often ones that are well-matched, such as fourths and sevenths (a seventh is the same distance as two consecutive fourths).

Bars 1-2

The initial fifth intervals are grouped into four-note structures and create a "4 against 3" feel when played as 1/8th-note triplets.

Bars 3-4

From the end of bar two we play a series of tenths. This section is typical of the sort of counterpoint that would sound best if the lead guitar was unaccompanied. In this setting, most listeners will just hear the melody traced out by the higher notes. Try to listen out for the low notes on the recording and not just the spikey high ones.

Bar 5

Each three-note motif in this bar is built from a seventh and fourth interval. Because they are arranged as nested tuplets, the right-hand taps beat out a 1/4 note triplet rhythm.

Bar 6

This passage uses a combination of right- and left-hand tapping, with each beat demonstrating two different ways of playing a fifth (on the same string and then across adjacent strings).

Bars 7-8

The same approach is also used here, only this time using tenths and sixths. Note the different motion of each four-note motif compared to bar 6.

Bars 9-11

Here we're playing fourths. This symmetrical approach can also be seen in bars 21-22, 42-43 and 44.

Bars 17-20

I took quite a loose rhythmic approach when recording this section and the results are transcribed so that you can see how this kind of flowing playing occurs intuitively. Note the tapped fifths reminiscent of Greg Howe.

Bars 21-22

This technical passage combines sweep picking, legato and slides. It focuses on a combination of fourths and fifths, which are inversions of each other and well matched.

Bar 23

This passage contains consecutive pairs of sixths played with both right- and left-hand tapping.

Bar 24

Simple but effective, the melody in the second half of this bar uses ascending thirds.

Bars 25-28 and (29-32)

This themed section involves repeated combinations of intervals:

- Bar 25 (29) = repeated octave + second + fifth pattern

- Bar 26 (30) = repeated octave + third + fourth pattern

- Bar 27 (31) = repeated octave + fourth + third pattern

- Bar 28 (32) = octave + fourth + second, followed by two ninths and a second

Bars 35-36

Now we play fourths using large stretches and string skips. The same approach is also taken in bars 41-43.

Bars 37-40

This passage contains melodies composed of various intervallic themes: seconds in bar 37, seconds and thirds in bar 38, fourths and seconds in bar 39, and seconds and thirds in bar 40.

Bars 45-47

This final section contains some different ways to mirror notes in the left hand with tapped notes in the right an octave higher.

MIND THE GAP
(Solo Study Featuring Mixed Intervals #1)

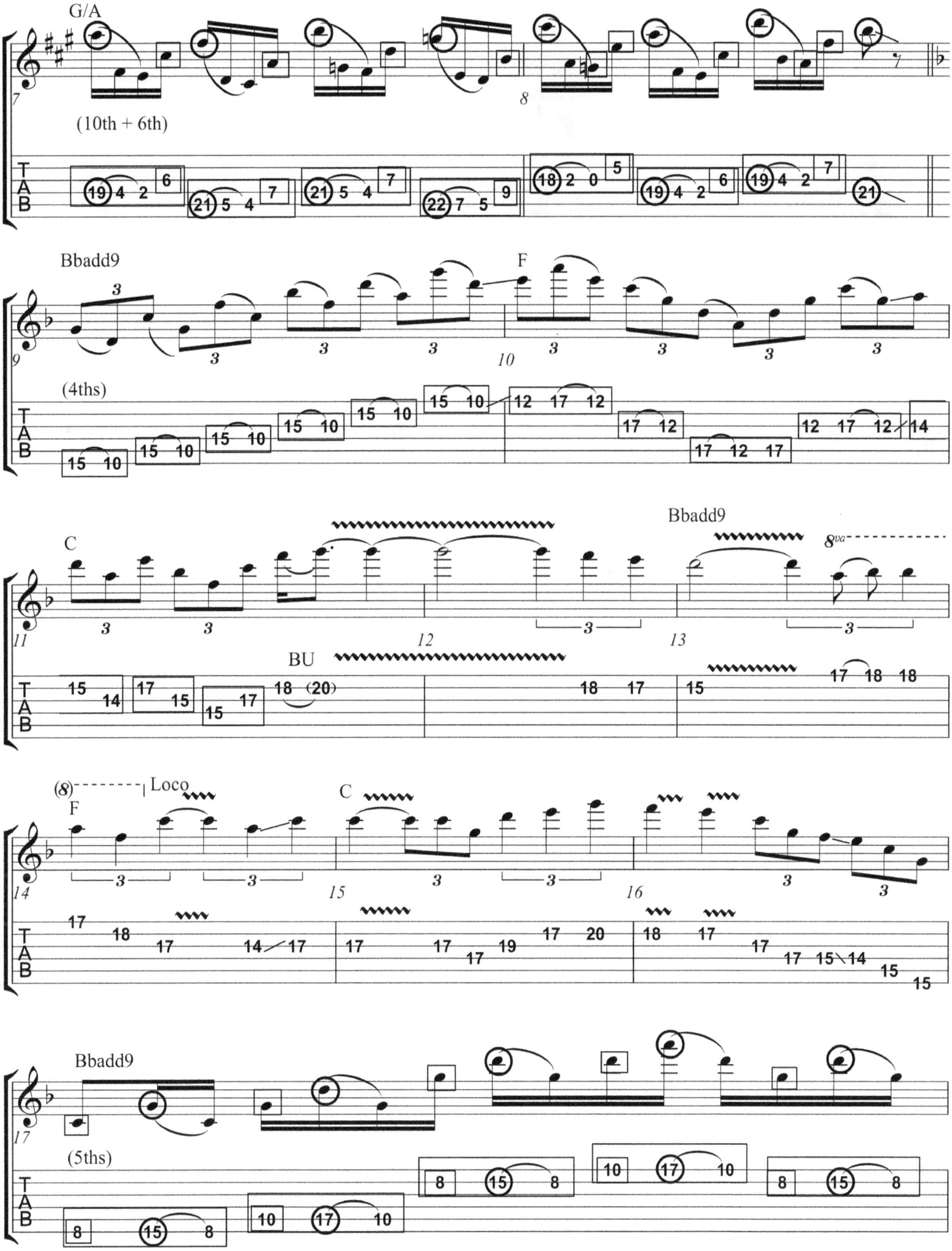
G/A
(10th + 6th)
Bbadd9
(4ths)
F
C
BU
Bbadd9
Loco
F
C
Bbadd9
(5ths)

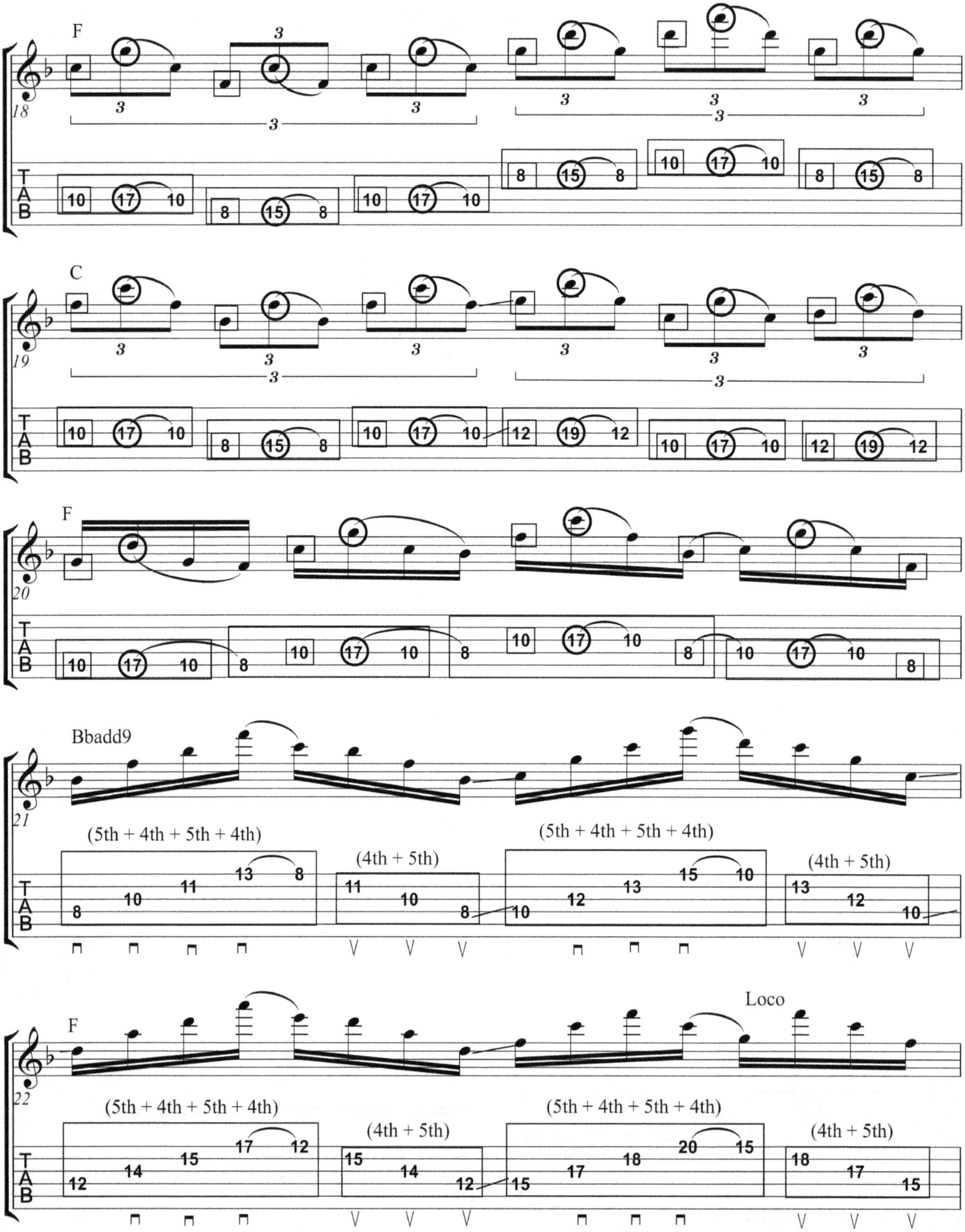
F
C
F
Bbadd9
(5th + 4th + 5th + 4th)
(4th + 5th)
(5th + 4th + 5th + 4th)
(4th + 5th)
F
Loco
(5th + 4th + 5th + 4th)
(4th + 5th)
(5th + 4th + 5th + 4th)
(4th + 5th)

C
23
(6ths)
24
Gliss. vib.
(3rds)
8va
A
25, 29
26, 30
Oct.
2nd
5th
3rd
4th
(8)
G/A
27, 31
28, 32
9ths
Loco
Bbadd9
F
33
34
(5th + 4th + 5th + 4th)
(4th + 5th)
(5th)

Loco
C
8va
(4ths)
(4ths + 5ths)
Loco
Bbadd9
F
C
(2nds)
(3rds)
(4ths)
(2nds)
8va
Loco
Bbadd9
(3rds)
(4ths)
F
C
Bbadd9
8va
(Octave + 4ths)
(Octaves)

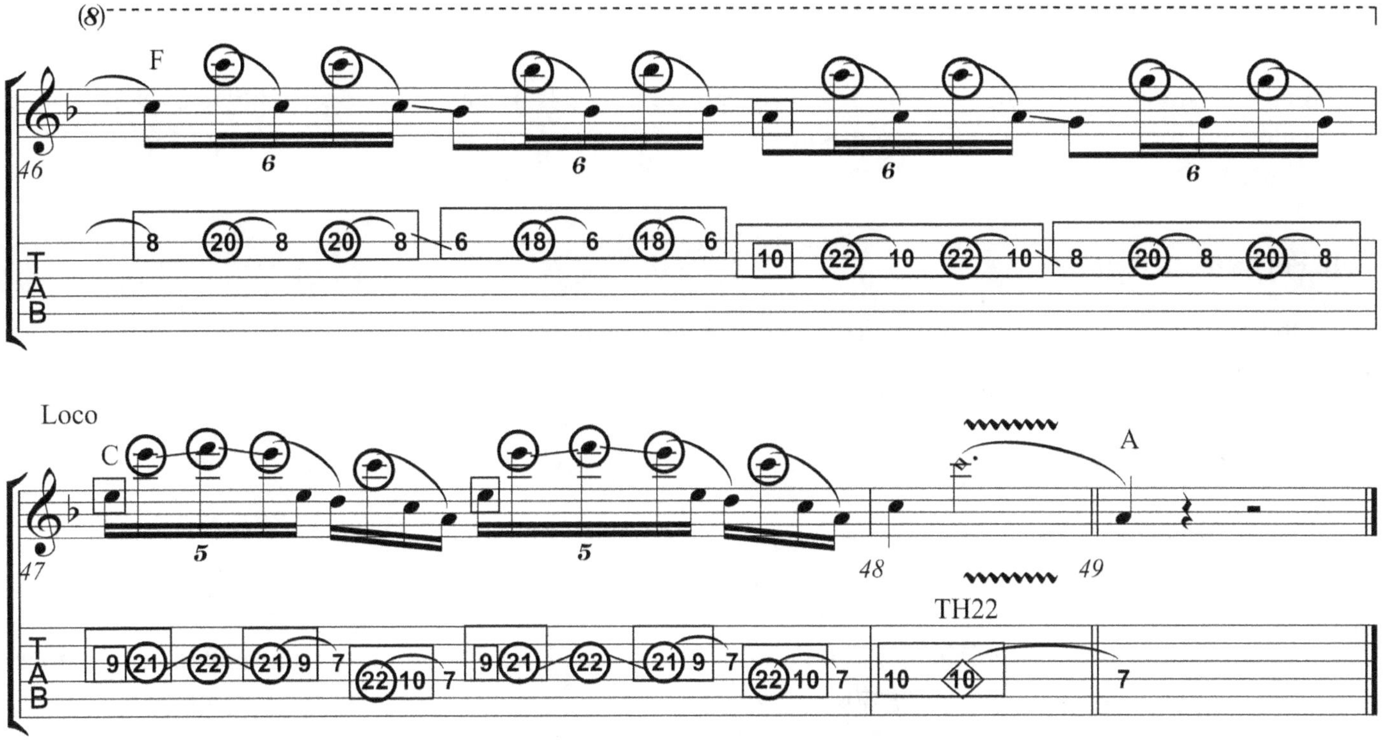
(8)
F
46
6
6
6
6
Loco
C
47
5
5
48
A
49
TH22

Chapter Ten: Mixed Intervals Solo Study Two

Our final solo study again combines simple and compound intervals. It's another opportunity to explore a more well-balanced approach to using these ideas in your own solos and compositions.

Solo Performance Notes

As in the previous solo some notes have rectangular boxes around them.

- Rectangle around two notes = a single diatonic interval

- Rectangle around three or more notes = multiple consecutive diatonic intervals

Bars 1-8

This opening riff features double-stopped seconds which contrast against the low palm-muted bass strings. Seconds sound gnarly when played together because they are so close in pitch that their frequencies clash in an arresting way – perfect for dark music like metal.

Bars 9-10

These two bars contain a series of diatonic triads. Normally, triads are formed of stacked thirds, but depending on what order you play the notes, there is also a fifth interval between the root and fifth.

Bars 11-12

More diatonic triads and arpeggios are played using consecutive thirds. I used sweep-picking to play this passage because the forms are so vertical. Aside from the first two notes, see if you can name the various triads and arpeggios formed throughout.

Bars 13-14

Hybrid picking is well-suited for the sevenths in these two bars but you can alternate pick if you prefer.

Bars 15-16

Conversely, you may want to use hybrid picking instead of economy picking for this consecutive sixths section. Although there are just as many awkward string skips as in the previous two bars, it's possible to pick everything because of all the slides and hammer-ons.

Using your first and second fingers works well, although it might not feel natural at first.

Bars 17-18

This single note, scale-based section helps to balance the solo.

I use left- and right-hand tapping for a smooth, even effect. However, you can use legato, picking or a combination of the two; whatever sounds good to you.

Bars 19-20

Now we combine left- and right-hand tapping on consecutive sevenths. Use two tapping fingers of the right hand – either the second and third fingers while holding the pick, or the first and second fingers if you can put the pick between your lips.

Bars 21-22

Here, each four-note structure is built from a diatonic tenth followed by a diatonic sixth.

Bars 23-24

As in bars 17-18, this passage also uses adjacent scale notes (seconds).

Bars 25-27

There is yet more left- and right-hand tapping here, this time to play a series of fifths. This passage was improvised, so looks a lot less metric than some of the other passages. If you experience difficulty reading the rhythms, just use your ears to get a sense of the flow and focus on destination points that are easy to hear.

Bar 30

Each three-note motif in this bar is a diatonic seventh that blends into a diatonic fourth.

Bar 31

The bend on the right-hand tap at the end of this passage of fifths is played by the left-hand at the 17th fret.

Bars 33-34

To contrast the note-density of some of the other passages, a short musical respite is provided by a scale melody using seconds.

Bars 35-36

Here there is some more melodic respite, mainly in the form of a Cadd11 arpeggio.

Bar 38

This ascending structure is built from three consecutive fourths and a third.

Bars 39-42

This melodic linking passage is composed mainly of seconds.

Bars 43-44

For a different texture, this section now features moving fifths against a stationary tapped pedal note.

Bars 47-48

This final arpeggio section uses a series of consecutive thirds. As in bars 11-12, see if you can name the various triads in this section.

TOUCHING THE VOID
(Solo Study Featuring Mixed Intervals #2)

(Shaun Baxter)

(Neck pick-up)
Bbadd9
F
(5ths + 3rds)
C
(Consecutive 3rds)
Bbadd9
8va
Loco
F
(7ths)
C
(consecutive 6ths)

(8)
Bbadd9
F
(consecutive 2nds)
(or pick)
Loco
C
(consecutive 7ths)
Bbadd9
F
(10ths + 6ths)
C
(2nds)
A
(5ths)

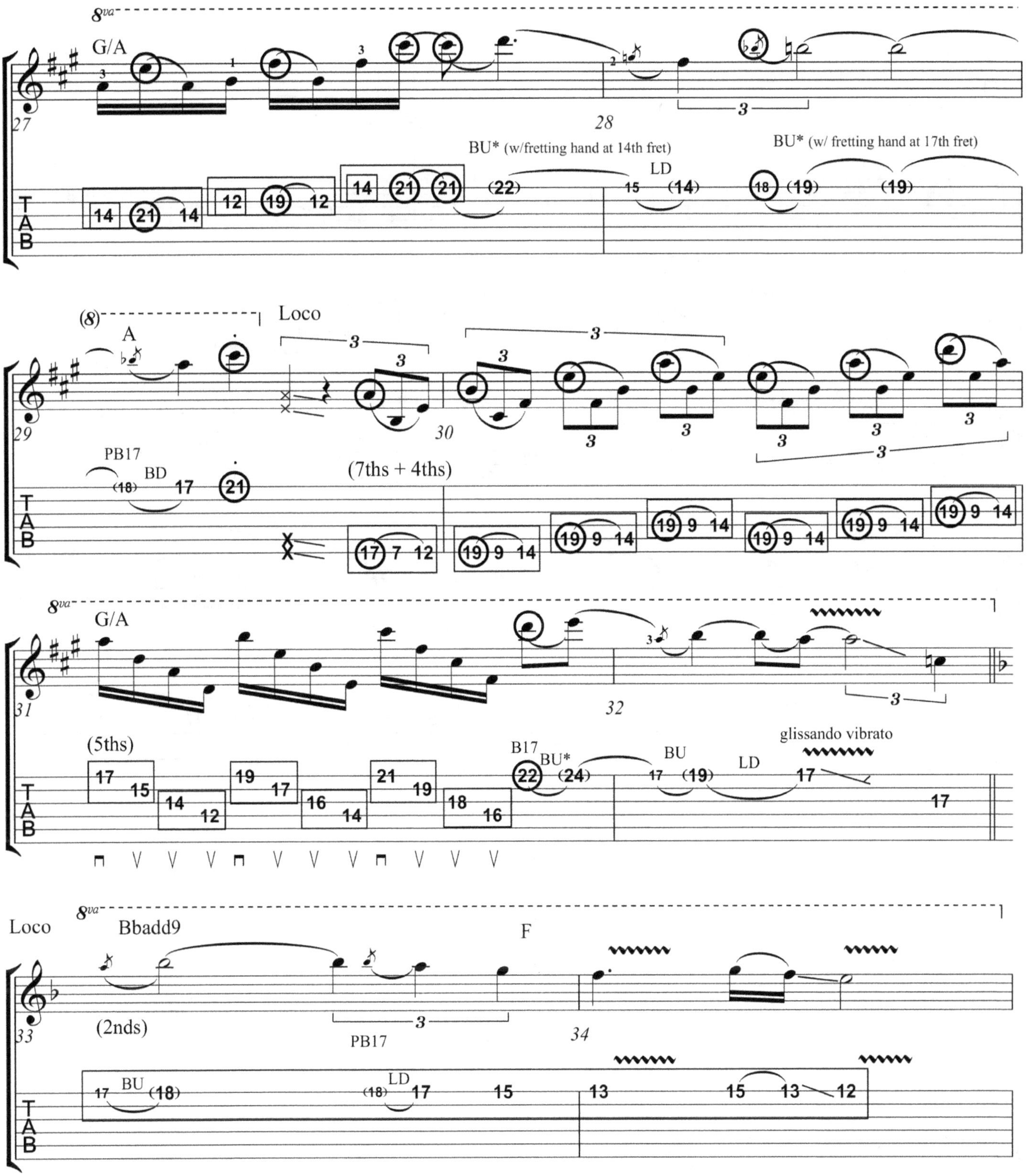
8va
G/A
27
28
BU* (w/fretting hand at 14th fret)
LD
BU* (w/ fretting hand at 17th fret)
(8)
A
Loco
29
30
PB17
BD
(7ths + 4ths)
8va
G/A
31
32
(5ths)
B17
BU*
BU
LD
glissando vibrato
Loco
8va
Bbadd9
F
33
34
(2nds)
PB17
BU
LD

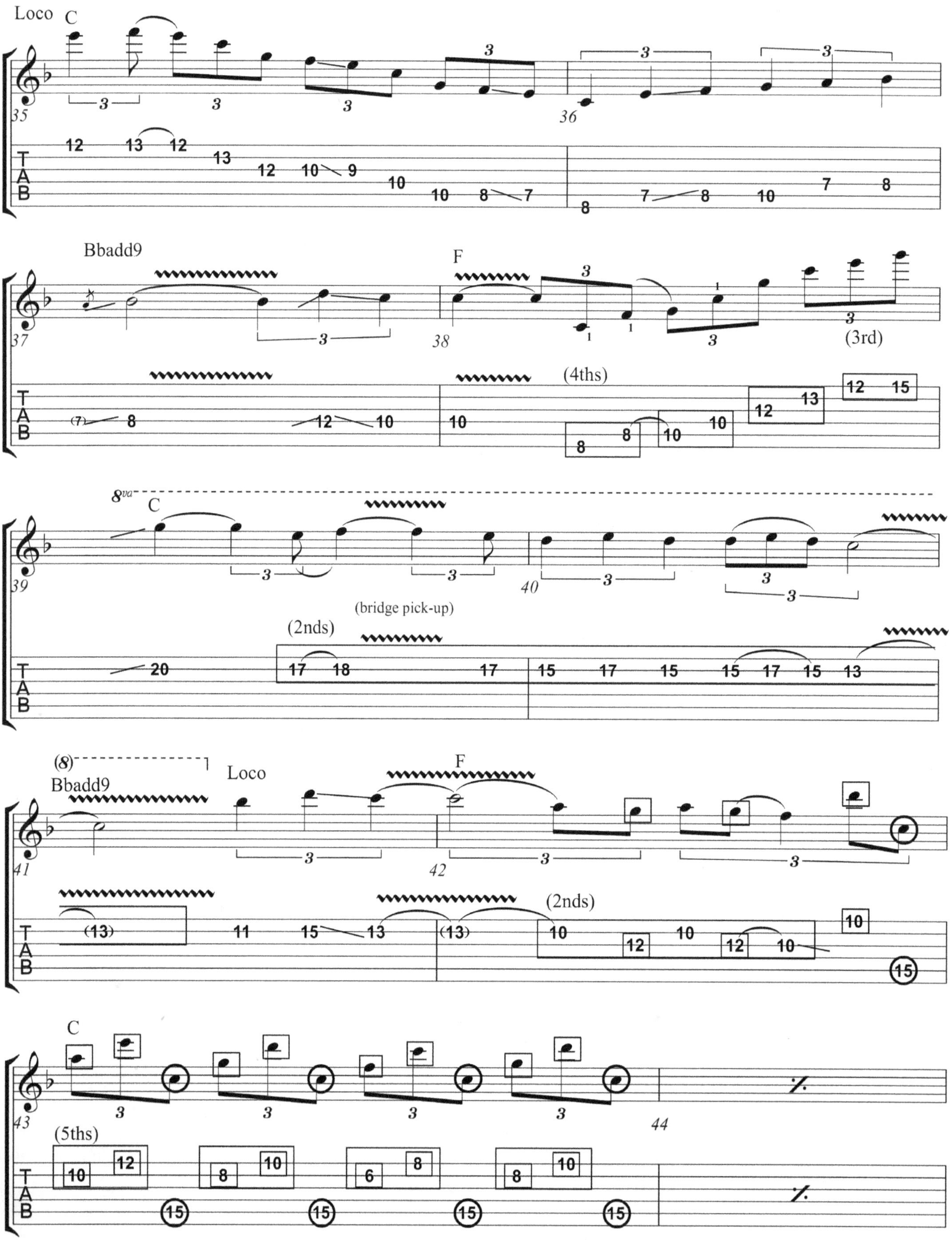
Loco
C
Bbadd9
F
(4ths)
(3rd)
8va
C
(bridge pick-up)
(2nds)
(8)
Bbadd9
Loco
F
(2nds)
C
(5ths)

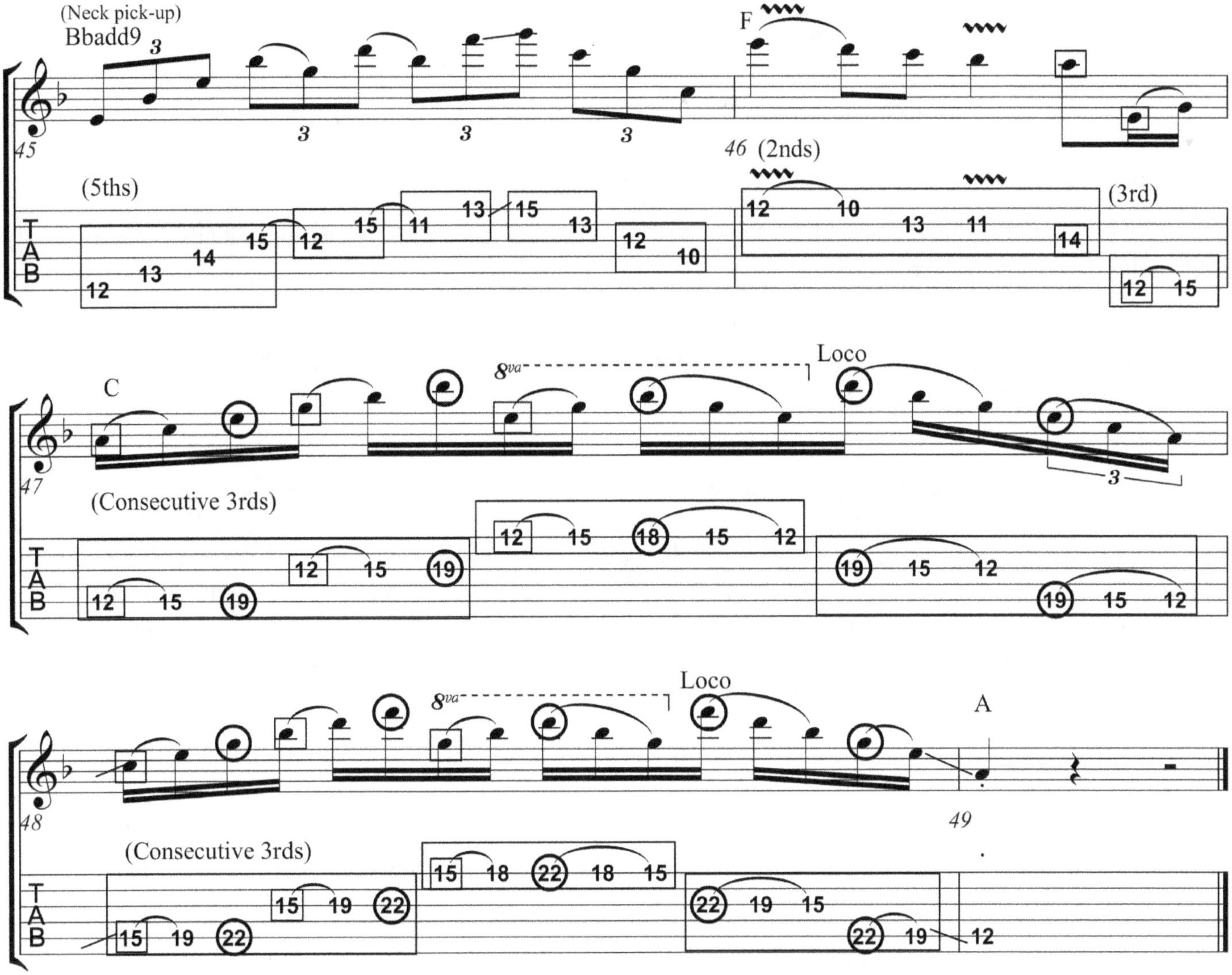
(Neck pick-up)
Bbadd9
F
(5ths)
(2nds)
(3rd)
C
Loco
(Consecutive 3rds)
Loco
(Consecutive 3rds)
A

Conclusion

I hope this book has helped you to understand intervals, see them in the scales you use, and appreciate them in terms of their inherent moods. If you want something sweet, use thirds, sixths and/or octaves; if you want something dark or dissonant, use something like sevenths.

My goal was to change how you look at scales, give you more ways to play them, and ideally help you apply these principles to any other scales you use.

Learning to shift ideas up and down the length of the neck, as well as staying in the same area, are both important areas of study, and you will get the most out of this book if you use the same principles to develop your own musical ideas. The aim is to build a useful, personalised repertoire to draw upon when forming your own sound.

Rather than trying to use every approach anywhere in any scale shape, I recommend that you maximise your chances of producing usable material by only using certain approaches in specific CAGED shapes where they fit comfortably. Using convenient patterns, then topping and tailing them so that you can flow in and out of them, is the healthiest way to approach this content. The truth is that some things are much easier to play in certain positions, so why waste your life trying to do something that's extremely difficult to pull off in a musical situation? Just go for the easy option. At least you'll be playing the idea somewhere, and there will always be *other* things to play in the other scale shapes.

Some Takeaways:

Adapt: be prepared to put in time to develop the technique required to play the ideas that you want to play.

Look for symmetry: when symmetrical shapes are available, use them! Beginning with the things that are easy to play, convenient, and quick to learn will allow you to get on with making music while other guitar players are waiting until they have also mastered all the difficult ones.

Two-notes-per-string: when using intervals such as fifths, octaves, tenths and thirteenths, it is often useful to arrange each scale as a series of two-note-per-string patterns.

Key-specific ideas: each solo represents a mini composition that demonstrates some of the many different possibilities provided by each interval type. Some of them feature key- or range-specific ideas (for example, ones that include open strings or wide stretches high on the neck). However, although such ideas will work well in a standalone composition, they will be less useful than ones that are transposable.

Capo: country guitar players play a lot of open string lines that are key-specific, but they often play songs in a limited range of keys and often use a capo to be able to continue to play their open string licks when an awkward key comes up. Depending on the music you play, you might want to do the same.

Similarly, you might want to consider a string damper – although the benefit of reduced unwanted noise will mean sacrificing the use of open strings.

Pentatonics: not all scales have seven notes, and you can produce some fantastic effects using the principles covered in this book applied to pentatonic scales. When you do this, it is probably best to think in terms of conventional intervals rather than pentatonic ones. For example, A to E would remain a fifth, even though E is four pentatonic notes from A (counting A as "1").

Final Thoughts

I would argue that if you only play what you hear in your head, you must have already heard it somewhere else for it to exist as an aural memory. However, one of the many merits of using music theory (including mathematical permutations) is that you can generate fresh ideas that work well but you have never heard before.

Working through these permutations can offer you the chance to create vocabulary that is truly original. And, once you start practicing such material, you will start getting used to the sound of notes being used in new ways. This, in turn, will allow you to hear them in your head when improvising. I've given a brief overview of my creation process in the Appendix that follows.

Finally, although it is important to be thorough and methodical to generate various ideas, the one thing that will knit them together and give them relevance is *expression*. Any scale, lick, line, or technique is useless to you if you cannot use it as a potential vehicle for self-expression.

Ultimately, your aim should be to transcend techniques and academic deliberation, so you can explore your own musical thoughts in an organic, emotional way.

Good luck!

Shaun

Appendix: Generating Material Systematically

In the introduction to this book I mentioned that I often explore a concept in forensic detail, to generate musical material that I then audition and retain or discard as my personal taste dictates. I'd like to take a moment to give you a brief overview of this process as it applies to intervals.

Note Configurations: Permutations and Fingerings

Permutations

There are various ways of generating material by exploring mathematical permutations. For example, there are six different ways of ordering three different pitches (where 1 is the lowest note and 3 is the highest):

123   132

213   231

312   321

And twenty-four ways of ordering four different pitches (where 1 is the lowest note and 4 is the highest):

1234   1243   1324   1342   1423   1432

2134   2143   2314   2341   2413   2431

3124   3142   3214   3241   3412   3421

4123   4132   4213   4231   4312   4321

I then audition these possibilities over my backing track (often by programming them into my sequencer / DAW without a guitar in my hands) to hear the ones that I like best.

I go through this process because it forces me to hear every possibility. I want to be thorough and ensure that I hear and experience all the material these sets of intervals can create.

From these ideas I choose my favourites, then work out ways to play them on the guitar.

The following is far from a complete list, but here are some ways of playing the four notes of an A7 arpeggio (A, C#, E, G) on the guitar.

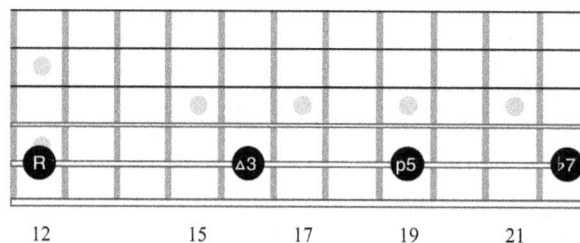

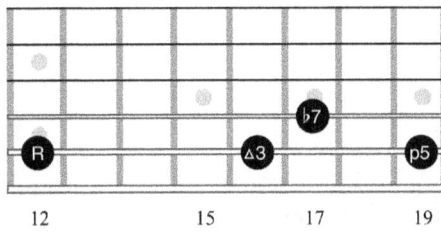

[3-1]

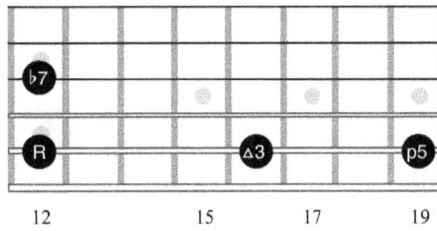

[3-1 with string-skip]

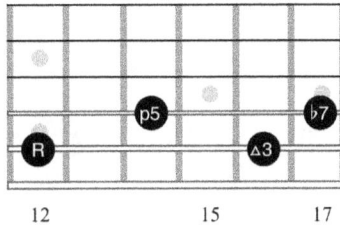

[2-2]

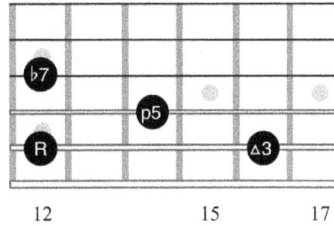

[2-1-1]

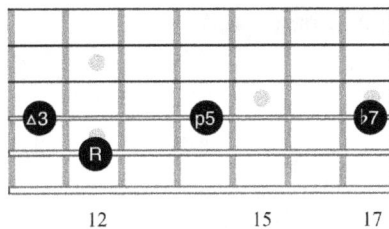

[1-3]

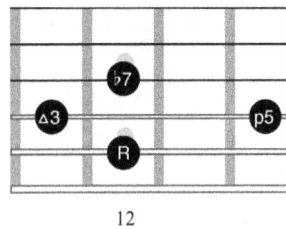

[1-2-1]

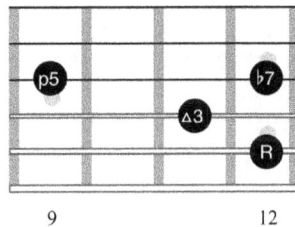

[1-1-2]

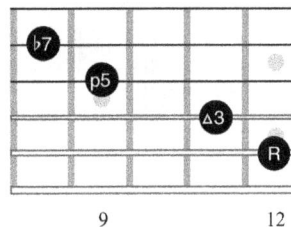

[1-1-1-1]

Once I've figured some note arrangements that I like the sound of, the next step is to find the best, or the most creative way to actually play them.

Here, I'm thinking about things like the basic approaches of legato vs picking or tapping, but also more subtle questions of finesse. For example:

- Would the line benefit from a slight amount of palm muting?

- Do I need to alter my picking style to get a more three-dimensional sound?

- Would everything sound cleaner if I used a string damper?

- Should there be a healthier balance between picked notes and legato notes.

- Are more expressive forms of articulation required, such as slides or vibrato?

- Are the dynamics even? Should some notes be accented?

As a composer and improvisor, these are the kinds of questions you should be asking yourself too. This is the stage at which those mathematical permutations become personal and musical.

As a working example, let's take just one of the 24 permutations shown above (3 2 1 4) applied to A7 with its notes configured 1-2-1 as follows:

A7 (1-2-1 Configuration)

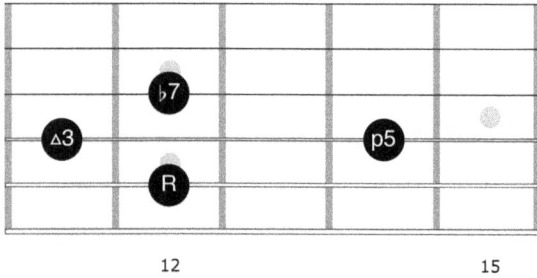

Here are just some of the various technical approaches that can be used:

a) A7   b) A7   c) A7   d) A7

e) A7   f) A7   g) A7

The thing is, although there are a lot of options here, it might be that you don't get on particularly well with *any* of them. In which case, the next step will be to re-finger things to broaden your technical options:

108

h) **A7** [4]   i) **A7** [1-3]   j) **A7** [2-2]

Pull-off to this from
right-hand tap on repeat.

k) **A7** [3-1]   l) **A7** [3-1 with string-skip]

m) **A7** [1-1-2]   n) **A7** [1-1-2]   o) **A7** [1-1-2]

Pull-off to this from
right-hand tap on repeat.

Pull-off to this from
right-hand tap on repeat.

p) **A7** [1-1-1-1]   q) **A7** [1-1-1-1]

Remember, your final choice on how a line should be fingered and technically performed will rely on a working compromise between the sound that you want to create and practicality (physical ease).

As you can see, this process is quite exhaustive and, although it's good to know that you've squeezed every drop of potential out of each concept, it is important to avoid becoming overwhelmed by the sheer volume of material that can be generated. *This is where editing is crucial!*

Remember, not every permutation sounds good (at least to you), so pick your favourites. It's possible that I'll explore thousands of ideas and potentially only end up with ten, but I know those ten ideas intimately. They become flexible friends that I learn to adapt in an infinite number of ways to fit any musical situation. Establishing vocabulary like this ensures that my improvisations are rooted in, and developed from, a thorough and highly personalised selection process.